Green Energy Pioneer

Kwame Martins's Solar Solutions

Jordan Hussain

ISBN: 9783100005520
Imprint: Telephasic Workshop
Copyright © 2024 Jordan Hussain.
All Rights Reserved.

Contents

Introduction

The world's energy crisis

Rising demand for energy

As the global population continues to grow at an unprecedented rate, the demand for energy has reached staggering levels. According to the International Energy Agency (IEA), global energy demand increased by approximately 2.3% in 2018 alone, with projections indicating that demand will continue to rise by 1.3% annually through 2040. This increasing demand poses significant challenges for energy production, distribution, and sustainability.

Factors Contributing to Increased Energy Demand

Several key factors contribute to the rising demand for energy:

- **Population Growth:** The world population is expected to reach nearly 10 billion by 2050, leading to an increased need for housing, transportation, and infrastructure, all of which require substantial energy resources.

- **Urbanization:** As more people move to urban areas, the concentration of populations in cities intensifies energy consumption. Urban centers are hotspots for energy use, driven by transportation, commercial activities, and residential needs.

- **Economic Development:** Developing nations are experiencing rapid industrialization, which significantly boosts energy demand. As countries like India and China continue to grow economically, their energy consumption per capita rises, leading to increased overall demand.

- **Technological Advancements:** Modern technologies, such as smartphones, electric vehicles, and smart appliances, require substantial energy to operate.

The proliferation of these technologies in everyday life adds to the energy demand.

Theoretical Framework: Energy Demand Models

To understand the dynamics of energy demand, several theoretical models are utilized. One such model is the *Kaya Identity*, which provides a framework for analyzing the factors that contribute to carbon emissions and energy consumption:

$$E = P \times \frac{E}{P} \times \frac{C}{E} \times \frac{E}{C} \tag{1}$$

Where:

+ E = total energy consumption

+ P = population

+ $\frac{E}{P}$ = energy use per capita

+ $\frac{C}{E}$ = carbon intensity of energy

+ $\frac{E}{C}$ = GDP per unit of energy

This identity illustrates how population growth, economic development, and energy efficiency interact to shape overall energy demand. As populations grow and economies develop, the challenge lies in decoupling energy consumption from carbon emissions to ensure sustainability.

Problems Associated with Rising Energy Demand

The rising demand for energy poses several critical problems:

+ **Resource Depletion:** Traditional energy sources, such as fossil fuels, are finite and are being consumed at an alarming rate. The extraction and use of these resources lead to depletion, making it imperative to find sustainable alternatives.

+ **Environmental Degradation:** Increased energy consumption from fossil fuels contributes to greenhouse gas emissions, air pollution, and climate change. The environmental impact of energy production is a pressing concern that necessitates a shift to cleaner energy sources.

- **Energy Security:** As countries compete for limited energy resources, energy security becomes a critical issue. Dependence on fossil fuel imports can lead to geopolitical tensions and economic vulnerabilities.

- **Infrastructure Strain:** The existing energy infrastructure in many regions is not equipped to handle the rising demand. Aging power grids and inadequate renewable energy integration can lead to power shortages and outages.

Examples of Rising Energy Demand

Several case studies illustrate the rising demand for energy across different regions:

- **China:** As the world's largest energy consumer, China's rapid industrialization has led to a dramatic increase in energy demand. The country is investing heavily in renewable energy sources to meet its growing needs while attempting to reduce its carbon footprint.

- **India:** With a population exceeding 1.3 billion, India's energy demand is projected to rise significantly. The government aims to expand its renewable energy capacity to 175 GW by 2022, highlighting the urgency of transitioning to sustainable energy solutions.

- **United States:** Although energy demand in the U.S. has stabilized in recent years, the rise of electric vehicles and increased reliance on digital technologies are expected to drive future demand. The transition to renewable energy sources is seen as a necessary step to mitigate the environmental impact of this growth.

In conclusion, the rising demand for energy is a multifaceted challenge that necessitates innovative solutions and a commitment to sustainability. As we delve deeper into the life and work of Kwame Martins, it becomes evident that addressing this demand through renewable energy technologies is not just a necessity but a moral imperative for future generations.

Environmental impact of traditional energy sources

The environmental impact of traditional energy sources, primarily fossil fuels such as coal, oil, and natural gas, is profound and multifaceted. The extraction, processing, and consumption of these energy sources contribute significantly to environmental degradation, climate change, and public health issues.

Greenhouse Gas Emissions

One of the most critical environmental impacts of traditional energy sources is the emission of greenhouse gases (GHGs). The combustion of fossil fuels releases carbon dioxide (CO_2), methane (CH_4), and nitrous oxide (N_2O) into the atmosphere. According to the Intergovernmental Panel on Climate Change (IPCC), energy production accounts for approximately 73% of total GHG emissions globally. The primary equation governing the relationship between fossil fuel consumption and CO_2 emissions can be expressed as:

$$E_{CO_2} = F \times EF \qquad (2)$$

where:

- E_{CO_2} = total CO_2 emissions (in tons),

- F = amount of fuel consumed (in gigajoules),

- EF = emissions factor (in tons of CO_2 per gigajoule).

For example, burning one ton of coal can release approximately 2.86 tons of CO_2 into the atmosphere. This significant increase in atmospheric CO_2 contributes to the greenhouse effect, leading to global warming and climate change.

Air Pollution

In addition to GHGs, the combustion of fossil fuels releases a variety of harmful air pollutants, including sulfur dioxide (SO_2), nitrogen oxides (NO_2), particulate matter (PM), and volatile organic compounds (VOCs). These pollutants have serious health implications, contributing to respiratory diseases, cardiovascular problems, and premature deaths. The World Health Organization (WHO) estimates that outdoor air pollution causes approximately 4.2 million premature deaths each year.

The formation of ground-level ozone, a secondary pollutant, is particularly concerning. When NO_2 reacts with sunlight, it forms ozone, which can cause respiratory issues and damage crops. The following reaction illustrates this process:

$$NO_2 + \text{sunlight} \rightarrow NO + O \qquad (3)$$

$$O + O_2 \rightarrow O_3 \qquad (4)$$

Water Pollution

The extraction and processing of fossil fuels also lead to significant water pollution. Hydraulic fracturing, or fracking, used to extract natural gas, can contaminate groundwater supplies with toxic chemicals. Oil spills, such as the Deepwater Horizon disaster in 2010, demonstrate the catastrophic effects of oil extraction on marine ecosystems. The spill released approximately 4.9 million barrels of oil into the Gulf of Mexico, severely impacting marine life and coastal communities.

Land Degradation and Habitat Loss

The infrastructure required for fossil fuel extraction, including drilling rigs, pipelines, and roads, often leads to habitat destruction and fragmentation. Deforestation for coal mining or oil extraction can result in the loss of biodiversity and disruption of ecosystems. The following equation represents the relationship between habitat loss (HL) and the area affected (A):

$$HL = A \times (1 - \text{Biodiversity Index}) \qquad (5)$$

where:

- HL = habitat loss,

- A = area affected (in hectares),

- Biodiversity Index = a measure of species richness and ecosystem health.

Climate Change and Extreme Weather Events

The cumulative effects of greenhouse gas emissions from traditional energy sources have led to climate change, which is associated with an increase in the frequency and severity of extreme weather events. Rising global temperatures contribute to more intense hurricanes, droughts, and floods. The economic costs of climate-related disasters are staggering, with the National Oceanic and Atmospheric Administration (NOAA) reporting that the U.S. experienced 22 separate billion-dollar weather and climate disasters in 2020 alone.

Conclusion

In summary, the environmental impact of traditional energy sources is extensive and detrimental. From greenhouse gas emissions and air pollution to water contamination and habitat destruction, the consequences of fossil fuel reliance are clear. Transitioning to renewable energy sources is not only a necessity for mitigating these impacts but also a crucial step toward ensuring a sustainable and healthy future for our planet.

The need for clean and renewable energy solutions

The urgency for clean and renewable energy solutions has never been more pronounced. As global energy demands continue to rise, so too does the environmental toll of traditional energy sources. This section will explore the pressing need for a transition to renewable energy, underpinned by theoretical frameworks, current challenges, and compelling examples.

Theoretical Framework

The concept of sustainability is foundational to understanding the need for renewable energy. The Brundtland Commission defined sustainable development as meeting the needs of the present without compromising the ability of future generations to meet their own needs [1]. This principle is critical when considering the finite nature of fossil fuels and their detrimental impact on the environment.

The energy transition theory posits that societies evolve through phases of energy consumption, moving from traditional biomass to fossil fuels, and eventually towards renewable energy sources [2]. This transition is not merely technological but also involves social, economic, and political dimensions. The current phase of energy consumption is characterized by a reliance on fossil fuels, which account for approximately 80% of global energy consumption [3].

Environmental Impact

The environmental impact of fossil fuel consumption is profound. The combustion of coal, oil, and natural gas releases significant amounts of carbon dioxide (CO_2) and other greenhouse gases into the atmosphere, contributing to climate change. The Intergovernmental Panel on Climate Change (IPCC) has highlighted that limiting global warming to 1.5°C above pre-industrial levels necessitates a reduction in CO_2 emissions of about 45% by 2030 and reaching net-zero by 2050 [4].

Mathematically, the relationship between CO_2 emissions and temperature rise can be expressed through the climate sensitivity parameter, which estimates the temperature increase in response to a doubling of atmospheric CO_2. This relationship is critical for understanding the urgency of transitioning to renewable energy sources, as illustrated by the equation:

$$\Delta T = \lambda \cdot \ln \left(\frac{C}{C_0} \right) \tag{6}$$

Where:

+ ΔT = change in temperature (°C)

+ λ = climate sensitivity parameter (°C per doubling of CO_2)

+ C = current concentration of CO_2

+ C_0 = pre-industrial concentration of CO_2

Economic Considerations

Transitioning to renewable energy is not only an environmental imperative but also an economic opportunity. According to the International Renewable Energy Agency (IRENA), renewable energy could create up to 24 million jobs globally by 2030 [5]. The declining costs of renewable technologies, particularly solar and wind, have made them competitive with fossil fuels. For instance, the cost of solar photovoltaic (PV) systems has dropped by 89% since 2009, making solar energy one of the cheapest sources of electricity [6].

Examples of Renewable Energy Solutions

Several countries have successfully implemented renewable energy solutions, showcasing the potential for a sustainable energy future. For example, Denmark has become a leader in wind energy, generating over 40% of its electricity from wind turbines [7]. Similarly, Germany's Energiewende (Energy Transition) policy aims to reduce greenhouse gas emissions by 55% by 2030, with a significant focus on expanding renewable energy sources [8].

In addition, innovative technologies such as energy storage systems, smart grids, and decentralized energy generation are transforming the energy landscape. For instance, Tesla's Powerwall allows homeowners to store solar energy for use during peak demand times, enhancing energy independence and reducing reliance on fossil fuels [9].

Conclusion

The need for clean and renewable energy solutions is underscored by the dual challenges of climate change and rising energy demand. The theoretical frameworks, environmental impacts, economic opportunities, and successful examples of renewable energy adoption illustrate the critical path forward. As we face an uncertain future, the transition to renewable energy is not just a choice; it is an imperative for the survival of our planet and the well-being of future generations.

Bibliography

[1] World Commission on Environment and Development. *Our Common Future.* Oxford University Press, 1987.

[2] Geels, F. W. "Regime Resistance Against Low-Carbon Transitions: Introducing Politics and Power in the Multi-Level Perspective." *Theory, Culture & Society*, vol. 31, no. 5, 2014, pp. 1-28.

[3] BP. "Statistical Review of World Energy 2021." BP, 2021.

[4] Intergovernmental Panel on Climate Change. "Global Warming of 1.5°C." IPCC, 2018.

[5] International Renewable Energy Agency. "World Energy Transitions Outlook 2020." IRENA, 2020.

[6] Lazard. "Lazard's Levelized Cost of Energy Analysis—Version 14.0." Lazard, 2020.

[7] Technical University of Denmark. "Wind Energy in Denmark." DTU, 2021.

[8] Federal Ministry for Economic Affairs and Energy. "Energiewende: Germany's Energy Transition." BMWi, 2020.

[9] Tesla, Inc. "Powerwall." Tesla, 2021.

The birth of Kwame Martins

Kwame's passion for science and technology

Kwame Martins was born into a world where the wonders of science and technology were not just subjects in school, but the very fabric of everyday life. Growing up in a modest neighborhood, he was surrounded by the hum of machinery, the flicker of computer screens, and the vibrant discussions of his family and friends about the latest technological advancements. This environment ignited a spark within him—a relentless curiosity about how things worked and a deep desire to contribute to a better future through innovation.

From an early age, Kwame was captivated by the principles of physics and chemistry. He often found himself dismantling household appliances, driven by an insatiable need to understand their inner workings. This hands-on experience was not merely a pastime; it was the foundation of his scientific education. He would often joke, "If you can't fix it, you don't really understand it." This philosophy guided him through his formative years, pushing him to embrace challenges and seek solutions.

Kwame's passion for science was further fueled by his participation in school science fairs and robotics competitions. These events were not just opportunities to showcase his projects; they were platforms for collaboration and innovation. He vividly remembers his first science fair project—a solar oven made from recycled materials. The project aimed to demonstrate how solar energy could be harnessed for cooking, and it won first place. This early success solidified his commitment to renewable energy and demonstrated the potential of using technology to solve real-world problems.

In high school, Kwame was fortunate to have a mentor, Mr. Thompson, who recognized his talent and passion for science. Mr. Thompson introduced him to advanced concepts in renewable energy, emphasizing the importance of sustainability in technology. Under his guidance, Kwame delved into the intricacies of solar energy, learning about photovoltaic cells and the physics behind converting sunlight into electricity. He became fascinated with the idea that the sun, a seemingly infinite source of energy, could be harnessed to power homes and businesses, reducing reliance on fossil fuels.

The theoretical foundations of solar energy intrigued Kwame. He learned that the efficiency of solar panels is often described by the equation:

$$\eta = \frac{P_{out}}{P_{in}} \times 100\% \tag{7}$$

where η is the efficiency, P_{out} is the electrical power output, and P_{in} is the solar power input. This relationship underscored the importance of improving solar technology to maximize energy conversion. Kwame often pondered the challenges faced in the industry, such as the cost of materials and the efficiency of conversion. He was determined to find solutions that would make solar energy more accessible and affordable.

Kwame's passion extended beyond theoretical knowledge; he was also deeply concerned about the environmental impact of traditional energy sources. He witnessed firsthand the effects of pollution in his community, from smog-filled skies to contaminated water sources. These observations fueled his desire to pursue a career in renewable energy, where he could contribute to a cleaner, healthier planet. He often engaged in discussions with peers about climate change, emphasizing that the transition to renewable energy was not just an option but a necessity for survival.

In college, Kwame's passion for science and technology blossomed into a full-fledged commitment to renewable energy. He immersed himself in courses on environmental science, electrical engineering, and sustainable development. He was particularly drawn to the concept of decentralized energy systems, which could empower communities to generate their own electricity. This idea resonated with him, as he envisioned a future where every household could harness solar power, reducing dependence on centralized energy grids.

Kwame's academic journey was not without challenges. He faced financial hurdles and the pressure of academic rigor, but his passion for science and technology kept him motivated. He often recalled the words of his mentor: "Passion is the fuel; perseverance is the engine." This mantra became his guiding principle, driving him to overcome obstacles and persist in his pursuit of knowledge.

In summary, Kwame Martins's passion for science and technology was shaped by a combination of early experiences, mentorship, and a deep-seated desire to effect positive change in the world. His journey from a curious child dismantling appliances to a determined innovator in the field of renewable energy is a testament to the transformative power of education and the relentless pursuit of one's passions. As he embarked on his journey to create Solar Solutions, he carried with him a wealth of knowledge, a network of support, and an unwavering commitment to a sustainable future.

Early influences and inspirations

Kwame Martins's journey into the world of renewable energy was not a solitary endeavor; it was profoundly shaped by a tapestry of early influences and inspirations that ignited his passion for science and technology. From a young age, Kwame found himself captivated by the wonders of the natural world and the potential for technology to harness these wonders for the benefit of humanity.

One of the most significant influences in Kwame's early life was his grandmother, who was a schoolteacher in their small community. She instilled in him a love for learning and a deep respect for the environment. Kwame recalls long afternoons spent in her garden, where she would explain the importance of plants in the ecosystem. This early exposure to nature's intricacies sparked a curiosity in Kwame that would later evolve into a commitment to sustainable practices.

Moreover, Kwame's upbringing in a region significantly affected by energy shortages provided him with firsthand experience of the challenges posed by traditional energy sources. The frequent power outages and reliance on fossil fuels for electricity made him acutely aware of the need for reliable and sustainable energy solutions. This experience would later serve as a driving force behind his commitment to renewable energy.

In high school, Kwame was fortunate to be mentored by Mr. Thompson, a passionate physics teacher who encouraged his students to think critically about the world around them. Mr. Thompson introduced Kwame to the principles of energy conversion and efficiency, emphasizing the importance of sustainable practices. One of the most memorable lessons involved a hands-on project where students built simple solar ovens. This project not only taught Kwame about solar energy but also showcased the practical applications of science in everyday life.

Theoretical foundations in physics, particularly the laws of thermodynamics, played a crucial role in shaping Kwame's understanding of energy systems. The first law of thermodynamics, which states that energy cannot be created or destroyed, only transformed, resonated with him as he contemplated how to harness renewable sources effectively. The equation representing this law can be expressed as:

$$\Delta U = Q - W \tag{8}$$

where ΔU is the change in internal energy, Q is the heat added to the system, and W is the work done by the system. This foundational principle guided Kwame in his quest to develop innovative solutions that would transform solar energy into usable power.

Additionally, Kwame's exposure to literature on environmental science significantly influenced his aspirations. Books such as *Silent Spring* by Rachel Carson and *The Uninhabitable Earth* by David Wallace-Wells opened his eyes to the urgent need for environmental stewardship and the dire consequences of inaction. These works not only educated him about the environmental crises facing the planet but also inspired him to become an advocate for change.

Kwame also sought inspiration from the stories of other innovators in the renewable energy sector. Figures like Elon Musk, who championed solar energy through his company SolarCity, and Wang Chuanfu, the founder of BYD, showcased the transformative power of innovation in addressing energy challenges. Their journeys illustrated the potential of perseverance and creativity in overcoming obstacles, further motivating Kwame to pursue his vision.

In conclusion, Kwame Martins's early influences and inspirations laid a robust foundation for his future endeavors in renewable energy. The combination of personal experiences, mentorship, theoretical knowledge, and the stories of other innovators collectively shaped his commitment to creating sustainable energy solutions. These influences not only fueled his passion but also equipped him with the tools necessary to navigate the complex landscape of the energy crisis, ultimately leading to the birth of Solar Solutions.

The importance of education in shaping his future

Education plays a pivotal role in shaping the trajectory of an individual's life, particularly for innovators like Kwame Martins. It serves not only as a vehicle for acquiring knowledge but also as a catalyst for personal growth, critical thinking, and problem-solving skills essential for addressing complex challenges such as the global energy crisis.

The Foundation of Knowledge

Kwame's educational journey began in a modest environment where access to resources was limited. However, his innate curiosity and passion for science drove him to seek knowledge beyond the classroom. Research has shown that early exposure to STEM (Science, Technology, Engineering, and Mathematics) can significantly influence a student's career path. According to a study by the National Math and Science Initiative (NMSI), students engaged in STEM education are more likely to pursue careers in these fields, which are crucial for innovation and economic growth [?].

Kwame's early fascination with renewable energy was ignited by a high school project on solar energy. This project not only provided him with foundational knowledge but also instilled a sense of responsibility towards environmental stewardship. As articulated in the works of educational theorist John Dewey, experiential learning is vital in fostering a deeper understanding of complex subjects. Dewey posited that education should be rooted in real-life experiences, enabling students to connect theory with practice [?].

Overcoming Barriers

Despite his enthusiasm, Kwame faced numerous obstacles on his educational journey, particularly financial constraints. Many students from underprivileged backgrounds encounter similar challenges, which can deter them from pursuing higher education. According to the College Board, nearly 30% of first-generation college students cite financial issues as a significant barrier to their educational aspirations [?]. Kwame's determination to overcome these barriers exemplifies the resilience often required to succeed in the face of adversity.

To navigate these challenges, Kwame sought scholarships and financial aid, emphasizing the importance of accessible education. The role of mentorship in education cannot be overstated; Kwame found guidance from teachers and community leaders who recognized his potential. Mentorship has been shown to enhance academic performance and increase the likelihood of college attendance among students from disadvantaged backgrounds [?].

The Role of Higher Education

Kwame's decision to pursue a degree in environmental science was a strategic choice that aligned with his vision of a sustainable future. Higher education provides individuals with specialized knowledge and skills that are crucial for innovation. A report by the National Science Foundation indicates that individuals with degrees in science and engineering are more likely to contribute to technological advancements and economic development [?].

During his time at university, Kwame engaged in research projects that focused on solar technology, allowing him to apply theoretical concepts in practical settings. This hands-on experience is vital for fostering innovation, as it enables students to experiment, fail, and ultimately succeed in developing new solutions. The concept of "learning by doing," as proposed by Dewey, underscores the importance of experiential learning in higher education [?].

Building a Network

Education also facilitated Kwame's ability to build a network of like-minded individuals and professionals in the renewable energy sector. Networking is a critical component of career development, as it opens doors to collaboration, funding opportunities, and mentorship. Research indicates that professional networks can significantly enhance career prospects, particularly in innovative fields [?].

Kwame participated in various conferences and workshops, where he connected with industry leaders and fellow innovators. These interactions not only expanded his knowledge but also inspired him to think creatively about the challenges facing the renewable energy sector. The importance of collaboration in innovation is supported by studies showing that diverse teams are more effective in problem-solving and generating new ideas [?].

Conclusion

In conclusion, education played a transformative role in shaping Kwame Martins's future as a green energy pioneer. It provided him with the knowledge, skills, and networks necessary to innovate in the field of renewable energy. Kwame's journey illustrates the profound impact that education can have on personal and professional development, particularly in addressing pressing global challenges. As we look towards the future, it is essential to advocate for equitable access to education, ensuring that aspiring innovators like Kwame can realize their potential and contribute to a sustainable world.

Chapter One: The Dream Begins

Kwame's journey to college

Overcoming financial challenges

Kwame Martins's journey towards becoming a green energy pioneer was fraught with financial obstacles. Growing up in a modest household, Kwame's family often struggled to make ends meet, which instilled in him a profound understanding of the value of money and the importance of financial planning. This section explores the various financial challenges he faced and the strategies he employed to overcome them.

Understanding the Financial Landscape

The financial landscape for aspiring innovators in the renewable energy sector can be daunting. According to the *International Renewable Energy Agency (IRENA)*, the initial capital investment required for renewable energy projects can be significantly higher than traditional energy sources. This is primarily due to the cost of research and development, prototyping, and the establishment of production facilities. For Kwame, this meant that pursuing his passion for solar energy would require not only innovative ideas but also a solid financial strategy.

Identifying Available Resources

Kwame began his journey by identifying various resources that could provide financial support. These included:

+ **Scholarships and Grants:** Kwame applied for numerous scholarships aimed at students pursuing degrees in science and technology. Notably, he was awarded the *Green Energy Scholarship*, which provided him with crucial funding for his education.

+ **Crowdfunding:** Recognizing the potential of crowdfunding platforms, Kwame launched a campaign to raise initial funds for his solar panel prototypes. He utilized platforms like *Kickstarter* and *GoFundMe*, where he shared his vision and attracted small investors who believed in his mission.

+ **Angel Investors:** Through networking events and industry conferences, Kwame connected with angel investors interested in supporting sustainable technologies. These investors provided not only capital but also mentorship and guidance.

Budgeting and Financial Planning

To navigate his financial challenges effectively, Kwame developed a comprehensive budgeting plan. This plan included:

$$\text{Total Expenses} = \text{Tuition Fees} + \text{Living Costs} + \text{Research Expenses} + \text{Prototyping Costs} \tag{9}$$

Kwame meticulously tracked his expenses and income, ensuring that he lived within his means while allocating sufficient funds for his projects. He often worked part-time jobs, balancing his studies with work to alleviate financial strain. This experience not only taught him the importance of financial discipline but also provided him with valuable insights into the operational side of running a business.

Leveraging Educational Opportunities

Kwame recognized that education was a powerful tool in overcoming financial barriers. He took advantage of every opportunity available to him, including:

+ **Internships:** Securing internships at renewable energy companies allowed him to gain practical experience while earning a stipend. These internships not only enhanced his resume but also expanded his professional network.

+ **Research Projects:** Participating in research projects funded by his university provided him with access to resources and funding that he could leverage for his solar panel development.

Building a Support Network

Kwame understood that he could not navigate these financial challenges alone. He actively sought out mentors and advisors who could provide guidance and support. By building a network of like-minded individuals, he was able to share resources, knowledge, and opportunities. This network proved invaluable, as many of his mentors had faced similar challenges and were willing to share their experiences and solutions.

Conclusion

Overcoming financial challenges was a critical component of Kwame Martins's journey to becoming a green energy pioneer. Through strategic planning, resource identification, and building a supportive network, he was able to navigate the financial landscape that often deters aspiring innovators. His story serves as a testament to the importance of resilience and creativity in the face of adversity, and it highlights the potential for success when one is willing to seek out and utilize available resources effectively.

Finding mentors and support networks

Kwame Martins's journey toward becoming a green energy pioneer was significantly influenced by the mentors and support networks he encountered along the way. The importance of mentorship in personal and professional development cannot be overstated; it serves as a catalyst for growth, providing guidance, knowledge, and encouragement. For Kwame, finding the right mentors was crucial in navigating the complexities of renewable energy, especially during his formative years in college.

The Role of Mentorship

Mentorship is defined as a relationship in which a more experienced or knowledgeable individual guides a less experienced person. According to Kram (1985), mentorship can be divided into two main functions: career support and psychosocial support. Career support includes sponsorship, exposure, coaching, and protection, while psychosocial support encompasses friendship, acceptance, and confirmation of identity.

Kwame's mentors provided both types of support, helping him to build confidence and develop the necessary skills to succeed in the renewable energy sector. For instance, during his early college years, he met Dr. Sarah Thompson, a renowned environmental scientist.   Dr.   Thompson not only guided him academically but also introduced him to industry contacts that would later prove invaluable.

Building a Support Network

In addition to finding mentors, Kwame recognized the importance of building a robust support network.   Networking is the act of establishing and nurturing mutually beneficial relationships with individuals who can provide support, information, and resources.   According to Granovetter (1973), weak ties—acquaintances rather than close friends—can be particularly valuable in providing new information and opportunities.

Kwame actively participated in various student organizations focused on sustainability and renewable energy.   Through these organizations, he met other like-minded individuals who shared his passion for green energy. This network not only provided emotional support but also facilitated collaborative projects and initiatives.   For example, Kwame and his peers organized a campus-wide solar energy awareness campaign, which attracted the attention of local businesses and potential investors.

Challenges in Finding Mentors

Despite the advantages of mentorship and networking, Kwame faced challenges in identifying suitable mentors. One significant barrier was the lack of representation of minority groups in the renewable energy sector.   Research indicates that individuals from underrepresented backgrounds often experience difficulties in accessing mentorship opportunities (Bennett et al., 2017).

Kwame's determination to overcome these obstacles led him to seek mentors outside of his immediate environment.   He utilized online platforms such as LinkedIn to connect with professionals in the renewable energy field.   This proactive approach allowed him to engage with experts and gain insights that would shape his understanding of the industry.

The Impact of Mentorship on Kwame's Development

The support Kwame received from his mentors and network had a profound impact on his personal and professional development.   For instance, during a pivotal moment in his academic career, Kwame was struggling with a challenging project on solar panel efficiency. His mentor, Dr. Thompson, encouraged him to approach the problem from a different angle, suggesting he explore innovative materials that could enhance the performance of solar panels. This guidance led to a breakthrough that not only improved his project but also laid the groundwork for his future endeavors.

Furthermore, Kwame's mentors instilled in him the importance of giving back to the community. Inspired by their example, he began mentoring younger students, sharing his knowledge and experiences in renewable energy. This cycle of mentorship not only reinforced his learning but also contributed to a growing community of passionate individuals dedicated to the pursuit of sustainable solutions.

Conclusion

In conclusion, finding mentors and building a support network were essential components of Kwame Martins's journey toward becoming a green energy pioneer. The guidance and encouragement he received from his mentors helped him navigate the challenges of the renewable energy sector, while his support network provided the collaborative environment necessary for innovation. As Kwame continued to grow and evolve in his career, he remained committed to fostering mentorship relationships, understanding that the power of connection is vital in the fight for a sustainable future.

Choosing a focus on renewable energy

Kwame Martins's decision to focus on renewable energy during his college years was not merely a matter of personal interest; it was a response to the pressing global energy crisis and the urgent need for sustainable solutions. This section explores the theoretical frameworks, challenges, and examples that influenced his academic and professional trajectory towards renewable energy.

Theoretical Framework

The foundation of Kwame's focus on renewable energy is rooted in several critical theories that highlight the importance of sustainable development. One such theory is the **Sustainable Development Goals (SDGs)**, established by the United Nations, which aim to address global challenges, including climate change, environmental degradation, and energy poverty. Goal 7 specifically emphasizes the need for access to affordable, reliable, sustainable, and modern energy for all.

Additionally, the **Energy Transition Theory** posits that societies must transition from fossil fuel dependency to renewable energy sources to mitigate climate change and promote environmental sustainability. This theory encompasses several stages, including the introduction of renewable technologies, the establishment of supportive policies, and the eventual societal acceptance and integration of these technologies.

Identifying Problems

Kwame was acutely aware of the problems associated with traditional energy sources. The reliance on fossil fuels has led to significant environmental degradation, including air and water pollution, habitat destruction, and greenhouse gas emissions. The **Intergovernmental Panel on Climate Change (IPCC)** has reported that the burning of fossil fuels is the largest single source of global greenhouse gas emissions, contributing to climate change and its associated impacts, such as extreme weather events and rising sea levels.

Furthermore, the concept of **energy poverty** became central to Kwame's focus. According to the World Bank, approximately 789 million people worldwide lack access to electricity. This lack of access exacerbates poverty and limits opportunities for education, healthcare, and economic development. Kwame understood that renewable energy solutions could provide a pathway to alleviate energy poverty while also addressing environmental concerns.

Examples of Renewable Energy Innovations

During his studies, Kwame was inspired by various examples of successful renewable energy projects that demonstrated the viability and effectiveness of these technologies. Notably, the **Solar Impulse Project**, which aimed to fly around the world using only solar power, showcased the potential of solar energy as a viable alternative to fossil fuels. The project not only highlighted the technological advancements in solar panel efficiency but also raised awareness about the importance of sustainable energy solutions.

Another influential example was the **Masdar City** initiative in Abu Dhabi, which aimed to be one of the most sustainable urban developments in the world. This project incorporated renewable energy sources, including solar and wind, as well as innovative energy efficiency measures. Masdar City served as a model for how urban planning could integrate renewable energy solutions to create sustainable living environments.

The Role of Education and Research

Kwame's commitment to renewable energy was further solidified through his academic pursuits. He sought out courses in environmental science, engineering, and policy, recognizing the interdisciplinary nature of renewable energy solutions. Engaging in research projects related to solar energy technology, Kwame was able to contribute to the development of more efficient solar panels and energy storage systems.

One significant project involved the analysis of the **Efficiency of Photovoltaic Cells**, where Kwame applied the following equation to understand the efficiency of solar panels:

$$\eta = \frac{P_{out}}{P_{in}} \times 100\%$$

where η is the efficiency, P_{out} is the output power of the solar panel, and P_{in} is the input power from sunlight. This research not only deepened his understanding of solar technology but also reinforced his belief in the potential of renewable energy to transform the energy landscape.

Conclusion

Kwame Martins's decision to focus on renewable energy was shaped by a combination of theoretical frameworks, recognition of global energy challenges, and inspiration from successful innovations. His educational journey equipped him with the knowledge and skills necessary to contribute to the renewable energy sector, setting the stage for his future endeavors in creating sustainable energy solutions. As he moved forward, Kwame remained committed to advocating for renewable energy as a key component in addressing the world's energy crisis and fostering a sustainable future.

The creation of Solar Solutions

Kwame's vision for a sustainable future

Kwame Martins envisions a world where clean, renewable energy is not just an alternative but the primary source of power for all human activities. His vision is rooted in the understanding that the current trajectory of energy consumption is unsustainable, leading to dire environmental consequences, economic disparity, and social injustice. To articulate this vision, Kwame draws upon several key principles of sustainability, which he believes should guide the development and implementation of renewable energy technologies.

The Triple Bottom Line

At the core of Kwame's vision is the concept of the Triple Bottom Line (TBL), which emphasizes the importance of balancing environmental, social, and economic factors. This holistic approach requires that any sustainable energy solution must not only reduce carbon emissions but also foster social equity and economic viability. Kwame often quotes the TBL framework, stating:

> "Sustainability is not just about saving the planet; it's about saving humanity and ensuring that future generations can thrive."

Decentralization of Energy Production

A significant aspect of Kwame's vision is the decentralization of energy production. He believes that energy should be generated as close to the point of use as possible, reducing transmission losses and enhancing energy security. By empowering local communities to harness solar energy, Kwame envisions a future where energy independence is achievable. This concept is supported by the following equation, which illustrates the potential reduction in transmission losses:

$$\text{Transmission Loss} = \frac{P_{\text{generated}} - P_{\text{used}}}{P_{\text{generated}}} \times 100\% \qquad (10)$$

Where $P_{\text{generated}}$ is the power generated at the source, and P_{used} is the power consumed. By decentralizing energy production, communities can significantly lower transmission losses, making energy use more efficient.

Integration of Technology and Nature

Kwame also emphasizes the importance of integrating technology with natural systems. He advocates for innovations that mimic natural processes, a concept known as biomimicry. For instance, he points to the development of solar panels that replicate the photosynthesis process in plants, enhancing efficiency and reducing waste. This integration can be mathematically represented by the efficiency equation for solar panels:

$$\eta = \frac{P_{\text{out}}}{P_{\text{in}}} \times 100\% \qquad (11)$$

Where η is the efficiency, P_{out} is the output power of the solar panel, and P_{in} is the input solar power. By increasing the efficiency of solar panels through innovative designs, Kwame envisions a future where solar energy can compete directly with fossil fuels.

Community Empowerment and Education

Kwame believes that for a sustainable future to be realized, it is essential to empower communities through education and involvement in renewable energy projects. He often shares stories of grassroots initiatives where local populations are trained to install and maintain solar systems, creating jobs and fostering a sense of ownership. This empowerment leads to a greater understanding of energy systems and encourages responsible energy consumption.

> "When communities understand the technology and its benefits, they become advocates for change, driving the transition to renewable energy from the ground up."

Policy Advocacy and Global Collaboration

Kwame's vision extends beyond local initiatives; he understands that systemic change requires robust policy frameworks and global collaboration. He actively engages with policymakers to advocate for incentives that support renewable energy adoption, such as tax credits for solar installations and funding for research in sustainable technologies. He emphasizes that effective policy can create a conducive environment for innovation and investment in green energy solutions.

Conclusion

In summary, Kwame Martins's vision for a sustainable future is multifaceted, incorporating principles of the Triple Bottom Line, decentralization of energy production, technological integration with nature, community empowerment, and policy advocacy. He believes that by embracing these principles, society can transition towards a more sustainable and equitable energy landscape, ultimately leading to a healthier planet and a brighter future for all. As Kwame often reminds his team:

> "The future is not something we enter; the future is something we create."

Prototyping and testing solar panels

The journey of creating effective solar panels begins with the prototyping phase, where theoretical concepts are transformed into tangible products. This phase is critical, as it allows innovators like Kwame Martins to test their ideas and refine them based on empirical data.

Theoretical Foundations

Solar panels operate on the principle of converting sunlight into electricity through the photovoltaic effect. When light photons strike the surface of a solar cell, they can dislodge electrons from atoms, creating a flow of electric current. The basic equation governing this process can be expressed as:

$$P = IV \tag{12}$$

where P is the power output in watts, I is the current in amperes, and V is the voltage in volts. The efficiency of a solar panel, which is a critical measure of its performance, is defined as the ratio of the electrical output to the incident solar energy, mathematically represented as:

$$\eta = \frac{P_{out}}{P_{in}} \times 100\% \tag{13}$$

where η is the efficiency, P_{out} is the electrical power output, and P_{in} is the power of the sunlight incident on the panel.

Prototyping Process

The prototyping process involves several stages:

+ **Material Selection:** Choosing the right materials is crucial. Common materials include monocrystalline silicon, polycrystalline silicon, and thin-film technologies. Each has its own set of advantages and disadvantages in terms of efficiency, cost, and manufacturing complexity.

+ **Design:** The design of the solar panel must optimize light absorption while minimizing resistive losses. This involves determining the optimal thickness of the semiconductor layer and the arrangement of the cells within the panel.

+ **Fabrication:** Once the design is finalized, the fabrication process begins. This typically involves doping silicon wafers with impurities to create p-n junctions, which are essential for the photovoltaic effect.

+ **Assembly:** The individual solar cells are then assembled into a panel. This includes connecting the cells in series and parallel configurations to achieve the desired voltage and current output.

Testing Methodologies

Testing solar panels is essential to ensure they meet performance standards and reliability. Several methodologies are utilized:

- **Performance Testing:** Panels are tested under standard test conditions (STC), which include a solar irradiance of 1000 W/m^2, a cell temperature of 25°C, and an air mass of 1.5. The output power is measured to determine efficiency.

- **Durability Testing:** Panels undergo stress tests to evaluate their durability against environmental factors such as extreme temperatures, humidity, and hail. Tests may include thermal cycling, damp heat, and mechanical load tests.

- **Field Testing:** Real-world performance is assessed by installing prototypes in various locations to monitor their output over time. This data helps identify any discrepancies between laboratory and actual performance.

Common Problems Encountered

During the prototyping and testing phases, several challenges may arise:

- **Efficiency Limitations:** Initial prototypes often exhibit lower efficiency than anticipated. This may be due to suboptimal material choices or design flaws that lead to increased resistive losses.

- **Manufacturing Defects:** Issues such as cracks in the silicon wafers or poor connections between cells can significantly affect the performance of the solar panel.

- **Environmental Impact:** The choice of materials and the manufacturing process can have environmental implications. It is essential to consider the lifecycle impact of the materials used.

Examples of Successful Prototyping

Kwame Martins and his team faced numerous challenges during the prototyping phase of Solar Solutions. One notable example was their development of a bifacial solar panel that could capture sunlight from both sides. This innovation was born out of the need to maximize energy capture, especially in areas with high albedo, such as deserts or snowy regions.

The initial prototypes were tested in various locations, including urban rooftops and rural areas. The results showed a remarkable increase in energy output compared to traditional monofacial panels, validating Kwame's vision for a more efficient solar solution.

Furthermore, through collaboration with local universities, Kwame's team was able to leverage advanced materials research, resulting in the incorporation of perovskite materials into their designs. This led to prototypes that not only reduced costs but also improved efficiency, demonstrating the potential for future innovations in solar technology.

In conclusion, the prototyping and testing phase is a critical component in the journey toward creating effective solar panels. By addressing theoretical principles, employing rigorous testing methodologies, and overcoming common challenges, innovators like Kwame Martins can make significant strides in the field of renewable energy. The insights gained from this phase not only contribute to the development of superior solar technologies but also lay the groundwork for a sustainable energy future.

Securing initial funding for the project

Securing initial funding is one of the most critical steps in transforming an innovative idea into a viable business. For Kwame Martins, the journey to fund his solar solutions project involved navigating a landscape that was both challenging and competitive. In this section, we will explore the various avenues Kwame pursued to secure the necessary financial backing, the theoretical underpinnings of funding acquisition, and real-world examples that illustrate the principles at play.

Understanding Funding Sources

When it comes to funding a startup, innovators typically explore several sources, which can be categorized into three primary types: **equity financing**, **debt financing**, and **grants**.

+ **Equity Financing** involves raising capital through the sale of shares in the company. Investors receive ownership stakes and, in return, expect to share in the profits and growth of the business. This can be particularly attractive for high-risk ventures like solar energy startups.

+ **Debt Financing** refers to borrowing money that must be repaid over time, typically with interest. This can come from banks, credit unions, or private lenders. While it allows the founder to retain full ownership, it imposes a financial burden that can be daunting for early-stage companies.

+ **Grants** are funds provided by governments, foundations, or other organizations that do not need to be repaid. These are often tied to specific projects or initiatives, particularly in sectors like renewable energy that align with public policy goals.

Kwame's strategy involved a mix of these funding sources, tailored to the unique needs of his solar solutions project.

Developing a Business Plan

A crucial component of securing funding is the development of a comprehensive business plan. This document serves not only as a roadmap for the business but also as a persuasive tool to attract investors. Key elements of a successful business plan include:

+ **Executive Summary:** A concise overview of the business, its mission, and its vision.

+ **Market Analysis:** An in-depth analysis of the solar energy market, including size, growth potential, and competitive landscape. For example, Kwame identified a growing demand for clean energy solutions, particularly in urban areas where traditional energy sources were becoming increasingly unsustainable.

+ **Financial Projections:** Detailed financial forecasts, including projected revenue, expenses, and profitability. A common approach is to utilize the following equation to estimate revenue:

$$\text{Revenue} = \text{Price per Unit} \times \text{Number of Units Sold} \qquad (14)$$

Kwame projected that with an initial investment, he could sell 10,000 solar panels in the first year at a price of \$200 each, leading to anticipated revenue of:

$$\text{Revenue} = 200 \times 10,000 = 2,000,000 \qquad (15)$$

+ **Funding Requirements:** A clear outline of how much funding is needed, how it will be used, and the expected return on investment for potential backers.

Networking and Pitching

Kwame understood the importance of networking in the funding process. He actively sought opportunities to connect with potential investors, mentors, and industry experts. This included attending renewable energy conferences, participating in pitch competitions, and leveraging platforms like LinkedIn to reach out to individuals in the venture capital space.

When it came time to pitch his project, Kwame focused on crafting a compelling narrative that highlighted the urgency of the energy crisis and the innovative nature of his solar solutions. He utilized the **elevator pitch** technique, which is a succinct and persuasive sales pitch that can be delivered in the time it takes to ride an elevator. This approach allowed him to quickly capture the interest of potential investors.

Overcoming Challenges

Despite his efforts, Kwame faced several challenges in securing funding. One of the primary obstacles was the skepticism surrounding solar energy investments. Many traditional investors were hesitant to back renewable energy projects, viewing them as high-risk ventures with uncertain returns.

To counter this skepticism, Kwame focused on presenting data and case studies that demonstrated the successful implementation of solar energy solutions in similar markets. He highlighted examples such as:

- **SolarCity**, which successfully grew by providing solar energy solutions to homeowners and businesses across the United States.

- **First Solar**, a leading manufacturer of solar panels that has consistently reported strong financial performance and growth in a competitive market.

These examples served to reassure potential investors of the viability of his project and the growing trend toward renewable energy adoption.

Conclusion

Securing initial funding for Solar Solutions was a multifaceted endeavor for Kwame Martins. Through a combination of equity financing, debt financing, and grants, along with a well-developed business plan, effective networking, and strategic pitching, he was able to attract the necessary capital to launch his innovative solar energy project. The challenges he faced only strengthened his resolve and commitment to creating a sustainable future through renewable energy.

As Kwame often reflected, the journey of funding is not just about the money; it is about building relationships and fostering a shared vision for a better world.

Assembling a team of like-minded individuals

In the journey of developing Solar Solutions, one of the most critical steps for Kwame Martins was assembling a team of like-minded individuals who shared his vision for a sustainable future. The importance of teamwork in innovation cannot be overstated, as diverse perspectives and expertise often lead to breakthroughs that an individual might not achieve alone.

Identifying Core Values and Vision

The first step in assembling his team was to identify individuals who resonated with his core values of sustainability, innovation, and social responsibility. Kwame understood that aligning on a shared vision was essential for fostering a collaborative environment. He articulated his vision through a mission statement that emphasized the need for clean energy solutions to combat climate change, stating:

$$\text{Vision} = \text{Sustainability} + \text{Innovation} + \text{Community Empowerment} \quad (16)$$

This equation not only encapsulated his goals but also served as a guiding principle in the recruitment process.

Recruitment Strategies

Kwame utilized various recruitment strategies to attract talented individuals to his cause. He tapped into his network from college, reaching out to professors and fellow students who had shown an interest in renewable energy. Additionally, he attended industry conferences and seminars, where he met professionals who were equally passionate about green technology.

Networking played a crucial role in his recruitment efforts. For instance, during a renewable energy summit, Kwame met Dr. Lisa Chen, a materials scientist specializing in photovoltaic technology. Recognizing her expertise, he invited her to join his team, emphasizing the importance of interdisciplinary collaboration in overcoming the challenges of solar energy development.

Building a Diverse Team

Diversity was a key consideration in assembling the team. Kwame believed that a group with varied backgrounds, experiences, and skill sets would foster creativity and innovation. He sought out individuals not only from engineering and science but also from business, policy, and community organizing. This diverse approach allowed the team to tackle problems from multiple angles.

For example, while Dr. Chen focused on the technical aspects of solar panel efficiency, Maria Gonzalez, a social entrepreneur, worked on community outreach and education. Together, they developed a program that educated local communities about the benefits of solar energy, ensuring that the technology would be embraced rather than resisted.

Fostering a Collaborative Environment

Once the team was assembled, Kwame prioritized creating a collaborative environment. He implemented regular brainstorming sessions where team members could share ideas and challenge each other's thinking. This culture of open communication was vital for innovation, as it allowed for the free exchange of ideas and constructive feedback.

To facilitate collaboration, Kwame introduced tools such as project management software and collaborative platforms that enabled real-time communication. This was particularly important as the team expanded and began working remotely. The use of technology ensured that geographical barriers did not hinder their progress.

Establishing Roles and Responsibilities

With a diverse team in place, it was crucial to establish clear roles and responsibilities. Kwame recognized that while collaboration was essential, accountability was equally important. He conducted individual meetings to understand each member's strengths and interests, assigning roles that aligned with their expertise.

For instance, while Dr. Chen led the technical development of solar panels, Maria took charge of community engagement initiatives. By clearly defining roles, Kwame ensured that each team member could focus on their area of expertise, leading to increased productivity and innovation.

Encouraging Continuous Learning

Kwame understood that the field of renewable energy was constantly evolving, and continuous learning was vital for the team's success. He encouraged team members to pursue professional development opportunities, attend workshops, and stay updated on the latest research and technologies.

This commitment to learning not only enhanced the team's skills but also fostered a culture of curiosity and innovation. As a result, the team was able to adapt to new challenges and incorporate cutting-edge technologies into their projects.

Celebrating Achievements

Finally, Kwame recognized the importance of celebrating achievements, both big and small. He instituted regular team meetings to acknowledge individual contributions and collective milestones. This practice not only boosted morale but also reinforced the sense of community within the team.

For example, after successfully securing their first round of funding, Kwame organized a team celebration, highlighting each member's role in the achievement. This not only motivated the team but also solidified their commitment to the shared vision of Solar Solutions.

Conclusion

In conclusion, assembling a team of like-minded individuals was a pivotal moment in Kwame Martins's journey toward creating Solar Solutions. By identifying core values, fostering collaboration, establishing clear roles, encouraging continuous learning, and celebrating achievements, Kwame laid the foundation for a successful and innovative organization. The diverse perspectives and expertise of his team not only propelled the development of solar technology but also contributed to a broader movement towards sustainable energy solutions.

Chapter Two: Challenges and Breakthroughs

The hurdles of bringing solar energy to the mainstream

Skepticism and resistance from traditional energy companies

The transition from traditional energy sources to renewable energy, particularly solar power, has faced significant skepticism and resistance from established energy companies. This resistance stems from various factors, including economic interests, regulatory challenges, and a deeply entrenched cultural mindset within the energy sector.

Economic Interests

Traditional energy companies, which primarily rely on fossil fuels such as coal, oil, and natural gas, have substantial financial investments in their existing infrastructure. The shift to solar energy threatens to disrupt their business models, leading to a natural inclination to resist change. For instance, companies like ExxonMobil and Chevron have historically allocated billions of dollars toward oil exploration and extraction. As solar technology advances and becomes more cost-effective, these companies face the risk of stranded assets—investments that may lose value as renewable energy becomes the preferred choice.

The economic impact of this transition can be quantified using the concept of *Levelized Cost of Energy (LCOE)*, which represents the average cost per unit of electricity generated over the lifetime of an energy project. The LCOE for solar energy has been decreasing rapidly, making it increasingly competitive with fossil fuels. According to the International Renewable Energy Agency (IRENA), the global weighted average LCOE of solar photovoltaics fell by 89% between 2009 and 2020. This decline poses a direct threat to traditional energy companies, which may see their market share diminish as consumers and businesses shift toward cheaper, cleaner alternatives.

Regulatory Challenges

In addition to economic pressures, traditional energy companies often wield significant influence over regulatory frameworks. Lobbying efforts aimed at shaping energy policy can create an environment that favors fossil fuels over renewables. For example, in the United States, the fossil fuel industry has historically lobbied against tax incentives and subsidies for solar energy, arguing that such measures distort the market. This resistance can manifest in the form of legislation that limits solar installations, imposes tariffs on solar panels, or undermines net metering policies that allow homeowners to sell excess energy back to the grid.

A notable example of this resistance occurred in 2018 when the Trump administration imposed tariffs on imported solar panels, citing national security concerns. This decision was met with backlash from the solar industry, which argued that the tariffs would lead to job losses and increased costs for consumers. The Solar Energy Industries Association (SEIA) estimated that the tariffs could result in the loss of 23,000 jobs in the solar sector. Such regulatory hurdles not only hinder the growth of solar energy but also reinforce the skepticism surrounding its viability as a mainstream energy source.

Cultural Mindset

The cultural mindset within traditional energy companies plays a crucial role in the resistance to solar energy. Many executives and decision-makers have backgrounds rooted in fossil fuel industries, leading to a reluctance to embrace new technologies that challenge the status quo. This mindset is often characterized by a focus on short-term profits rather than long-term sustainability. As a result, companies may prioritize immediate financial returns over investments in renewable energy research and development.

Moreover, the narrative surrounding renewable energy has historically been framed as a fringe movement, often dismissed as impractical or unfeasible. This skepticism is perpetuated by media portrayals and public discourse that emphasize the challenges of renewable energy, such as intermittency and storage issues, while downplaying the rapid advancements being made in these areas. For instance, the development of battery storage technologies, such as lithium-ion batteries, has made significant strides in addressing the intermittency of solar energy, yet many traditional energy companies continue to overlook these innovations.

Conclusion

The skepticism and resistance from traditional energy companies toward solar energy present significant challenges for pioneers like Kwame Martins. However, as the economic, regulatory, and cultural landscapes evolve, there is potential for collaboration and innovation. By addressing these barriers and fostering a more inclusive dialogue between traditional and renewable energy sectors, a sustainable energy future can be realized. The journey toward widespread adoption of solar energy is fraught with obstacles, but it is essential for innovators to remain steadfast in their mission to create a cleaner, greener world.

Navigating complex regulations and policies

The transition to solar energy is not merely a technological challenge; it is also a complex regulatory landscape that innovators like Kwame Martins must navigate. Understanding the legal frameworks, incentives, and bureaucratic hurdles is essential for the successful implementation of solar solutions. This section explores the multifaceted nature of regulations affecting the solar energy sector, the challenges posed by these regulations, and the strategies employed to overcome them.

Understanding Regulatory Frameworks

Regulatory frameworks governing renewable energy vary significantly by region and country. In many cases, these regulations are designed to promote energy efficiency and sustainability. For instance, the **Public Utility Regulatory Policies Act (PURPA)** in the United States encourages the development of renewable energy by requiring utilities to purchase power from independent producers at favorable rates. However, the complexities arise from the myriad of regulations at the federal, state, and local levels.

Challenges in Compliance

One of the primary challenges faced by solar innovators is ensuring compliance with existing regulations. This often involves navigating a web of local zoning laws, building codes, and environmental regulations. For example, in some jurisdictions, solar installations may require permits that can take weeks or months to obtain, delaying project timelines. The following are key challenges in compliance:

+ **Zoning Laws:** Local governments may impose restrictions on where solar panels can be installed, affecting both residential and commercial projects. These laws can vary widely, creating confusion for developers.

+ **Interconnection Standards:** Connecting solar systems to the grid involves adhering to specific technical standards, which can differ from one utility to another. This inconsistency can complicate the integration of solar power into the existing energy infrastructure.

+ **Environmental Regulations:** Solar projects may need to undergo environmental impact assessments, particularly if they are large-scale installations. These assessments can be time-consuming and require significant resources.

Strategies for Navigating Regulations

To address these challenges, innovators like Kwame Martins often employ several strategies:

+ **Engaging with Policymakers:** Building relationships with local and state policymakers can facilitate smoother navigation of regulations. By actively participating in public hearings and consultations, innovators can advocate for more favorable policies and regulations.

+ **Utilizing Legal Expertise:** Hiring legal experts who specialize in energy regulations can help innovators understand the intricacies of compliance. These professionals can provide guidance on navigating the permitting process and help avoid potential legal pitfalls.

+ **Advocacy and Coalition Building:** Forming coalitions with other renewable energy stakeholders can amplify voices advocating for regulatory reform. By presenting a united front, these coalitions can influence policy changes that benefit the solar industry.

Case Study: Solar Solutions' Experience

Kwame Martins and his team at Solar Solutions encountered significant regulatory hurdles during their early days. For instance, while attempting to launch a community solar project in a suburban area, they faced stringent zoning restrictions that limited the installation of solar panels on residential rooftops.

To overcome this, they organized community meetings to educate residents about the benefits of solar energy and the potential economic advantages. By fostering community support, they were able to lobby local officials for a zoning variance that allowed for the installation of a community solar garden, ultimately paving the way for a successful project.

Conclusion

Navigating complex regulations and policies is a critical aspect of the renewable energy landscape. For innovators like Kwame Martins, understanding and effectively managing these challenges not only facilitates the growth of their ventures but also contributes to the broader adoption of solar energy. As the industry continues to evolve, ongoing advocacy for regulatory reform will be essential to creating a more conducive environment for renewable energy solutions.

$$E = mc^2 \tag{17}$$

This famous equation by Einstein symbolizes the transformative power of energy, paralleling the need for innovative approaches to harnessing clean energy in a regulatory landscape that often poses challenges. Just as Einstein's theory revolutionized physics, navigating and reforming energy regulations can revolutionize the solar energy sector and contribute to a sustainable future.

Raising awareness and educating the public about solar energy

As Kwame Martins embarked on his mission to promote solar energy, one of the most significant challenges he faced was the widespread lack of understanding and awareness regarding the benefits and feasibility of solar technology. The transition from traditional fossil fuels to renewable energy sources requires not just technological advancements but also a shift in public perception and behavior. This section explores the strategies employed by Kwame and his team to educate the public and raise awareness about solar energy.

Understanding the Knowledge Gap

The general public often harbors misconceptions about solar energy, viewing it as an expensive, complicated, or unreliable alternative to fossil fuels. A study conducted by the Solar Energy Industries Association (SEIA) found that nearly

70% of respondents were unaware of the financial incentives available for solar installations. This knowledge gap presents a significant barrier to the adoption of solar technology.

Educational Initiatives

To address this issue, Kwame initiated a series of educational campaigns aimed at demystifying solar energy. These initiatives included:

- **Workshops and Seminars:** Kwame organized community workshops where experts explained the basics of solar energy, its benefits, and how it can be integrated into everyday life. These sessions were designed to be interactive, allowing attendees to ask questions and engage directly with the material.

- **School Programs:** Partnering with local schools, Kwame introduced educational programs that taught students about renewable energy. By targeting younger generations, he aimed to foster a culture of sustainability that would carry into adulthood.

- **Online Resources:** Recognizing the power of digital media, Kwame's team created a comprehensive website filled with resources, including articles, videos, and infographics explaining solar technology. This platform served as a hub for information, making it easily accessible to the public.

Community Engagement

Engaging directly with the community was essential for raising awareness. Kwame implemented several strategies to create a dialogue around solar energy:

- **Solar Demonstration Projects:** By installing solar panels on community centers and schools, Kwame provided tangible examples of solar energy in action. These installations served as educational tools, allowing community members to see the technology firsthand and understand its benefits.

- **Collaborations with Local Influencers:** Partnering with respected community leaders and influencers helped to amplify the message. When local figures endorsed solar energy, it lent credibility to the initiative and encouraged more people to consider solar solutions.

+ **Public Events and Festivals:** Kwame organized solar fairs and participated in local festivals to showcase solar technology. These events featured interactive displays, live demonstrations, and opportunities for attendees to speak with experts about solar energy.

Utilizing Social Media and Digital Platforms

In the digital age, social media has become a powerful tool for education and awareness. Kwame leveraged platforms such as Facebook, Twitter, and Instagram to reach a broader audience. His strategies included:

+ **Informative Campaigns:** Creating shareable content that highlights the benefits of solar energy, such as cost savings, environmental impact, and energy independence. Infographics and short videos were particularly effective in capturing attention and conveying complex information quickly.

+ **Engagement through Q&A Sessions:** Hosting live Q&A sessions on social media allowed the public to ask questions directly, fostering a sense of community and addressing specific concerns about solar energy.

+ **Success Stories:** Sharing testimonials and case studies of individuals and businesses that successfully adopted solar energy helped to personalize the message and demonstrate real-world applications.

Overcoming Resistance and Misconceptions

Despite these efforts, resistance to solar energy persisted, often rooted in long-standing beliefs about fossil fuels. Kwame's approach to overcoming this resistance involved:

+ **Addressing Misconceptions Head-On:** By directly confronting common myths about solar energy—such as its reliability, cost, and efficiency—Kwame's team aimed to provide clear, evidence-based responses. For instance, they presented data showing that solar panels can produce energy even on cloudy days, thereby alleviating concerns about their effectiveness.

+ **Highlighting Financial Incentives:** Educating the public about available financial incentives, such as tax credits and rebates, was crucial. Kwame's team created easy-to-understand guides that outlined how individuals could benefit financially from switching to solar energy.

- **Demonstrating Long-Term Savings:** By providing calculations that illustrated the long-term savings associated with solar energy adoption, Kwame effectively shifted the focus from initial costs to lifetime benefits. The equation for calculating the return on investment (ROI) for solar energy can be expressed as:

$$\text{ROI} = \frac{\text{Total Savings} - \text{Initial Investment}}{\text{Initial Investment}} \times 100$$

This formula helped potential customers visualize the financial benefits over time.

The Role of Policy and Advocacy

Kwame understood that raising public awareness was not solely about education; it also required advocacy for supportive policies. He worked tirelessly to inform the public about the importance of government incentives and regulations that encourage solar energy adoption. This involved:

- **Lobbying for Renewable Energy Policies:** Engaging with local and state governments to advocate for policies that support renewable energy initiatives, such as net metering and feed-in tariffs.

- **Educating the Public on Policy Impacts:** Conducting informational sessions that explained how policies directly affect the community's ability to adopt solar energy. For example, he illustrated how tax credits could significantly reduce the upfront costs of solar panel installation.

Conclusion

Raising awareness and educating the public about solar energy was a multifaceted challenge that Kwame Martins approached with creativity and determination. Through workshops, community engagement, digital campaigns, and policy advocacy, he worked to bridge the knowledge gap and dispel misconceptions. By empowering individuals with information and resources, Kwame not only promoted solar energy but also inspired a movement towards a more sustainable future.

Innovations and breakthroughs in solar panel technology

Increasing efficiency and affordability

The quest for increasing the efficiency and affordability of solar panels is at the heart of Kwame Martins's mission with Solar Solutions. As the global demand for renewable energy surges, enhancing the performance of solar technologies while reducing costs becomes imperative. This section delves into the theoretical foundations, challenges faced, and innovative solutions that have emerged in the field of solar energy.

Theoretical Foundations

The efficiency of a solar panel is defined as the ratio of the electrical output to the incident solar energy. Mathematically, it can be expressed as:

$$\eta = \frac{P_{out}}{P_{in}} \times 100\% \tag{18}$$

where η is the efficiency, P_{out} is the electrical power output of the solar panel, and P_{in} is the solar power incident on the panel.

The maximum theoretical efficiency of a solar cell is determined by the Shockley-Queisser limit, which for a single-junction solar cell is approximately 33.7%. This limit arises from the fundamental physics of photon absorption and the energy bandgap of the semiconductor material used. To surpass this limit, researchers have explored multi-junction solar cells that stack multiple layers of materials, each designed to absorb different segments of the solar spectrum.

Challenges in Efficiency and Affordability

Despite the theoretical advancements, several challenges hinder the widespread adoption of high-efficiency solar technologies:

+ **Material Costs:** High-performance materials, such as gallium arsenide (GaAs), can be prohibitively expensive. This raises the overall cost of solar panels, making them less accessible to consumers and businesses.

+ **Manufacturing Processes:** The production of high-efficiency solar cells often involves complex manufacturing processes that require advanced technology and significant investment. This can lead to higher costs that are passed on to the end-user.

* **Market Competition:** Traditional silicon-based solar cells dominate the market due to their lower initial costs, despite their lower efficiency. This creates a challenging environment for newer technologies that aim for higher efficiency.

Innovative Solutions

To tackle these challenges, Kwame and his team at Solar Solutions have focused on several innovative strategies:

1.   **Advanced Materials:** The exploration of alternative materials, such as perovskite solar cells, has shown promise in enhancing efficiency while reducing costs. Perovskites can be produced using low-cost raw materials and have achieved efficiencies exceeding 25% in laboratory settings. Ongoing research aims to scale up production methods to make these materials commercially viable.

2. **Bifacial Solar Panels:** By utilizing bifacial solar panels, which capture sunlight from both sides, the overall energy yield can be significantly increased. This technology allows for greater energy production without a corresponding increase in cost, effectively lowering the cost per watt.

3.   **Innovative Manufacturing Techniques:** Employing new manufacturing techniques, such as roll-to-roll printing for thin-film solar cells, can drastically reduce production costs. This method allows for continuous production on flexible substrates, making it possible to manufacture solar panels at a fraction of the cost of traditional methods.

4. **Scale Economies:** As Solar Solutions expands its production capacity, the company benefits from economies of scale. Increased production leads to lower costs per unit, making solar energy more affordable for consumers. Strategic partnerships with other manufacturers further enhance production efficiency and cost-effectiveness.

Real-World Examples

Several real-world examples illustrate the successful application of these strategies:

+ **Perovskite Solar Cells:** Research institutions, such as the University of California, Berkeley, have developed perovskite cells that demonstrate high efficiencies and low production costs. Collaborations with industry partners are underway to bring these innovations to market.

+ **Bifacial Technology:** Major solar manufacturers, such as Trina Solar, have successfully commercialized bifacial solar panels, reporting up to 30% more energy generation compared to traditional panels in certain installations. This has led to increased adoption in both residential and commercial sectors.

+ **Thin-Film Solar Cells:** Companies like First Solar have pioneered thin-film technology, achieving significant cost reductions while maintaining competitive efficiency levels. Their manufacturing processes have set industry standards for affordability and sustainability.

Conclusion

Increasing the efficiency and affordability of solar panels is not merely an engineering challenge; it is a critical component of Kwame Martins's vision for a sustainable energy future. By leveraging advanced materials, innovative manufacturing techniques, and strategic partnerships, Solar Solutions is not only enhancing the performance of solar technology but also making it accessible to a broader audience. As the world transitions to renewable energy, the efforts to improve solar efficiency and affordability will play a pivotal role in shaping a cleaner, more sustainable future for all.

Exploring new materials and designs

The quest for more efficient solar panels has led researchers and innovators like Kwame Martins to explore new materials and designs that can significantly enhance the performance and reduce the costs of solar energy systems. This section delves into the various materials currently under investigation, their theoretical foundations, the challenges they present, and notable examples of successful implementations.

Theoretical Foundations of Solar Cell Materials

Solar cells operate based on the photovoltaic effect, where light energy is converted into electrical energy. The efficiency of this conversion is largely dependent on the materials used in the solar cells. Traditional silicon-based solar cells have dominated the market due to their relatively high efficiency and established manufacturing processes. However, the theoretical maximum efficiency of silicon solar cells is limited to about 29.4% according to the Shockley-Queisser limit [?]. This limit arises from the bandgap of silicon, which is approximately 1.1 eV.

To overcome these limitations, researchers are investigating alternative materials with different bandgaps that can capture a broader spectrum of sunlight. The ideal bandgap for solar energy conversion is around 1.34 eV, allowing for better absorption of the solar spectrum while minimizing thermal losses.

Emerging Materials

1. **Perovskite Solar Cells**: Perovskite materials, characterized by their unique crystal structure, have emerged as a promising alternative to silicon. They can be synthesized using low-cost materials and have shown remarkable efficiency improvements, reaching over 25% in laboratory settings [?]. The general formula for perovskite is ABX$_3$, where A is typically a cation such as methylammonium, B is a metal cation like lead, and X is a halide ion.

$$E_g = \frac{hc}{\lambda} \tag{19}$$

Where E_g is the bandgap energy, h is Planck's constant, c is the speed of light, and λ is the wavelength of light.

The challenge with perovskite solar cells lies in their stability and lead content, which raises environmental concerns. Researchers are actively working on lead-free alternatives and encapsulation techniques to enhance durability.

2. **Organic Photovoltaics (OPVs)**: Organic solar cells utilize organic molecules or polymers to absorb sunlight and generate electricity. They offer the advantage of being lightweight, flexible, and potentially cheaper to produce. The efficiency of OPVs has improved significantly, reaching around 18% [?].

OPVs operate on the principle of exciton generation, where absorbed photons create excitons (bound electron-hole pairs) that must be separated to generate current. The challenge lies in the relatively low charge mobility and stability of organic materials.

3. **Thin-Film Technologies**: Thin-film solar cells, such as Cadmium Telluride (CdTe) and Copper Indium Gallium Selenide (CIGS), are another area of exploration. These materials require less material than traditional silicon panels and can be deposited on flexible substrates. CdTe solar cells have reached efficiencies of around 22%, while CIGS has achieved up to 23.4% [?].

The primary challenges for thin-film technologies include material toxicity (especially with cadmium) and the need for efficient manufacturing processes that can scale up production.

Innovative Designs

In addition to exploring new materials, innovative designs are crucial for enhancing solar panel efficiency.

1. **Bifacial Solar Panels**: Bifacial panels can capture sunlight from both sides, increasing energy generation by utilizing reflected light from surfaces such as snow or sand. This design can boost energy output by 10-20% compared to traditional monofacial panels.

2. **Concentrated Photovoltaics (CPV)**: CPV systems use mirrors or lenses to focus sunlight onto small, high-efficiency solar cells. This approach can significantly increase the amount of solar energy captured, but it requires precise tracking systems to follow the sun's movement.

3. **Building-Integrated Photovoltaics (BIPV)**: BIPV incorporates solar cells into building materials such as windows and facades, providing aesthetic benefits while generating electricity. This design not only helps in energy generation but also reduces the overall energy consumption of buildings.

Challenges and Future Directions

Despite the promising developments in new materials and designs, several challenges remain. Stability and longevity of materials, manufacturing scalability, and cost-effectiveness are critical factors that need to be addressed. Moreover, the integration of these new technologies into existing energy systems requires collaboration between innovators, policymakers, and industry leaders.

The future of solar energy will likely involve a combination of various materials and designs, tailored to specific applications and environments. Continued research and investment in these areas will be essential for achieving a sustainable and efficient energy future.

Conclusion

Exploring new materials and designs is a vital component of advancing solar technology. As Kwame Martins and his team at Solar Solutions continue to innovate, they contribute to a growing body of knowledge that not only aims to enhance the efficiency of solar energy systems but also strives to make clean energy accessible to all. The journey towards sustainable energy solutions is ongoing, and the potential for breakthroughs in material science and engineering remains vast.

Addressing issues of scalability and storage

As the demand for solar energy solutions increases, the issues of scalability and energy storage become critical to the success and integration of solar technology into the energy grid. While solar energy has made significant strides in efficiency and affordability, the ability to scale production and store energy effectively remains a challenge that innovators like Kwame Martins must address.

Scalability Challenges

Scalability refers to the capacity to increase production and deployment of solar technology to meet rising energy demands. One of the primary challenges in scaling solar energy is the manufacturing process of solar panels. Traditional silicon-based solar cells, while efficient, require significant amounts of raw materials and energy to produce. The equation governing the efficiency of solar panels can be expressed as:

$$\eta = \frac{P_{out}}{P_{in}} \times 100 \tag{20}$$

where η is the efficiency, P_{out} is the electrical power output, and P_{in} is the solar power input. As demand increases, the need for higher efficiency and lower production costs becomes paramount.

Material Availability

The availability of raw materials poses another significant challenge. The production of silicon solar cells requires high-purity silicon, which is often sourced from limited geographical locations. Additionally, the extraction and processing of materials like silver and indium, used in various solar technologies, raise concerns about environmental impact and sustainability. Innovations such as perovskite solar cells, which utilize abundant materials, are promising alternatives that could alleviate some of these concerns. The efficiency of perovskite cells has been shown to approach that of traditional silicon cells, with reports indicating efficiencies exceeding 25% in laboratory settings.

Storage Solutions

Energy storage is another critical component of a scalable solar energy solution. Solar energy generation is intermittent, dependent on sunlight availability, which means that energy must be stored for use during non-generating hours. Current storage technologies primarily rely on lithium-ion batteries, which have limitations in terms of cost, lifespan, and environmental impact.

The energy storage capacity can be quantified using the following equation:

$$E_{storage} = C \times V \times t \tag{21}$$

where $E_{storage}$ is the total energy stored, C is the capacity of the battery (in ampere-hours), V is the voltage, and t is the time (in hours) the battery can deliver power. As Kwame Martins and his team explored alternative storage solutions, they considered options such as flow batteries, which offer longer discharge times and can be scaled more easily by increasing the size of the tanks that hold the electrolyte solution.

Innovative Approaches to Storage

To address the challenges of energy storage, several innovative approaches are being explored:

1. **Grid-scale Storage Solutions**: Systems such as pumped hydro storage (PHS) and compressed air energy storage (CAES) can store large amounts of energy for extended periods. PHS utilizes excess energy to pump water uphill to a reservoir, which can then be released to generate electricity when needed.

2. **Hydrogen Storage**: Another promising method is the conversion of excess solar energy into hydrogen through electrolysis. The reaction can be represented as:

$$2H_2O \rightarrow 2H_2 + O_2 \tag{22}$$

This hydrogen can then be stored and used as a fuel source or converted back into electricity in fuel cells.

3. **Innovative Battery Technologies**: Research into solid-state batteries and sodium-ion batteries offers potential solutions to the limitations of current lithium-ion technology. These alternatives promise greater energy density, lower costs, and improved safety profiles.

Real-world Examples

Several successful projects exemplify the integration of scalable solar solutions and energy storage. For instance, the Hornsdale Power Reserve in South Australia utilizes a large array of Tesla Powerpacks to store energy generated from solar farms, providing stability to the grid and offering services such as frequency control and demand response.

Similarly, Kwame Martins's Solar Solutions has partnered with local governments to implement community solar projects paired with battery storage systems. These projects not only provide renewable energy to underserved areas but also demonstrate the viability of scalable solar solutions in real-world applications.

Conclusion

Addressing the challenges of scalability and storage is essential for the future of solar energy. Through innovative technologies and strategic partnerships, Kwame Martins and his team are paving the way for a more sustainable and resilient energy landscape. By continuously improving the efficiency of solar panels and exploring diverse storage solutions, they are not only enhancing the viability of solar energy but also contributing to a cleaner, greener future for all.

Collaborating with other renewable energy innovators

Collaboration among renewable energy innovators is crucial for advancing technology and achieving a sustainable energy future. In the rapidly evolving landscape of clean energy, partnerships can lead to significant breakthroughs that no single entity could achieve alone. This section explores the importance of collaboration, the challenges faced, and notable examples of successful partnerships in the renewable energy sector.

The Importance of Collaboration

Collaboration in the renewable energy sector allows innovators to share resources, knowledge, and expertise. By working together, companies can leverage complementary strengths, reduce costs, and accelerate the development of new technologies. The combined efforts of multiple stakeholders can lead to enhanced research and development capabilities, resulting in improved efficiency and performance of renewable energy systems.

One key theoretical framework that supports the importance of collaboration is the concept of *open innovation*. Open innovation posits that firms can and should use external ideas and pathways to advance their technology. According to Chesbrough (2003), "open innovation is the use of purposive inflows and outflows of knowledge to accelerate internal innovation and expand the markets for external use of innovation." This theory underlines the necessity for renewable energy innovators to engage with external partners, including universities, research institutions, and other companies.

Challenges in Collaboration

Despite the benefits, collaboration in the renewable energy sector is not without challenges. Some of the common issues include:

- **Intellectual Property Concerns:** Companies may be hesitant to share proprietary information or technology due to fears of losing competitive advantage. Establishing clear agreements regarding intellectual property rights is essential for fostering trust among collaborators.

- **Cultural Differences:** Collaborators from different organizations may have varying corporate cultures, decision-making processes, and communication styles. These differences can lead to misunderstandings and hinder effective collaboration.

- **Resource Allocation:** Collaborating organizations must carefully manage the allocation of resources, including time, funding, and personnel. Disparities in resource commitment can create tension and affect project outcomes.

Addressing these challenges requires strong leadership, clear communication, and well-defined roles and responsibilities within collaborative projects.

Examples of Successful Collaboration

Several notable collaborations in the renewable energy sector have led to significant advancements in technology and market adoption.

1. SolarCity and Tesla   One of the most prominent examples is the partnership between SolarCity and Tesla. When SolarCity, a leading solar energy provider, merged with Tesla, the two companies combined their expertise in solar energy and battery storage. This collaboration resulted in the development of the Solar

Roof and the integration of solar energy systems with Tesla's Powerwall battery storage solutions. The synergy between these two innovators has not only enhanced the efficiency of solar energy systems but also made them more accessible to consumers.

2. The Solar Energy Research Institute of Singapore (SERIS) The Solar Energy Research Institute of Singapore (SERIS) collaborates with various international partners to advance solar energy technology. By engaging with universities, industry players, and government agencies, SERIS has developed innovative solar panel designs and improved energy efficiency. Their collaborative research has also focused on integrating solar energy with smart grid technologies, enhancing the overall effectiveness of renewable energy systems.

3. The Global Solar Council The Global Solar Council is an international organization that brings together solar energy stakeholders from around the world. By fostering collaboration among industry leaders, researchers, and policymakers, the council aims to promote the adoption of solar energy and advocate for favorable policies. Through joint initiatives and knowledge-sharing platforms, the Global Solar Council has played a pivotal role in accelerating the global transition to solar energy.

Conclusion

In conclusion, collaboration among renewable energy innovators is essential for overcoming the challenges of the energy crisis and advancing the adoption of clean energy technologies. By embracing open innovation principles and addressing the challenges of collaboration, stakeholders in the renewable energy sector can accelerate the development of sustainable solutions. The examples of successful partnerships, such as those between SolarCity and Tesla, SERIS, and the Global Solar Council, highlight the transformative potential of collaboration in driving the renewable energy movement forward. As Kwame Martins and his team at Solar Solutions continue to innovate, they must seek out and cultivate partnerships with other leaders in the field to maximize their impact on the green energy landscape.

Chapter Three: Sustaining Success

Scaling up Solar Solutions

Expanding production and distribution networks

As Kwame Martins's vision for Solar Solutions began to take shape, the necessity for a robust production and distribution network became apparent. The transition from a small-scale prototype to mass production was fraught with challenges, yet it was essential for meeting the rising demand for solar energy solutions. This section delves into the strategies employed by Kwame and his team to expand their production capabilities and distribution channels effectively.

Production Expansion Strategies

To increase production capacity, Solar Solutions adopted several key strategies:

1. **Automation of Manufacturing Processes:** One of the first steps taken was to invest in automated manufacturing technologies. By implementing robotic systems and automated assembly lines, the company could significantly reduce labor costs and increase production speed. The use of automation allowed for the consistent quality of solar panels, which is crucial for maintaining consumer trust and meeting regulatory standards. The equation for calculating the production efficiency can be expressed as:

$$E = \frac{P_a}{P_t} \times 100\% \qquad (23)$$

where E is the efficiency percentage, P_a is the actual production output, and P_t is the theoretical maximum output.

2. **Lean Manufacturing Techniques:** To minimize waste and optimize resource utilization, Solar Solutions adopted lean manufacturing principles. This approach involved streamlining the production process, reducing excess inventory, and improving workflow efficiency. Techniques such as Just-In-Time (JIT) inventory management were implemented, allowing the company to respond swiftly to market demands without overproducing.

3. **Scaling Up Facilities:** Expanding physical production facilities was another critical step. Kwame secured funding to build new manufacturing plants equipped with advanced technologies. These facilities were strategically located near key markets to reduce transportation costs and improve delivery times.

4. **Sourcing Sustainable Materials:** As part of their commitment to sustainability, Solar Solutions focused on sourcing materials that were not only cost-effective but also environmentally friendly. Establishing relationships with suppliers who prioritized sustainable practices ensured that the production process aligned with the company's green ethos.

Distribution Network Development

In tandem with production expansion, the development of a comprehensive distribution network was vital for reaching a broader customer base. The following strategies were employed:

1. **Partnerships with Distributors:** Kwame recognized the importance of forming strategic partnerships with established distributors. By collaborating with companies that had existing logistics and distribution networks, Solar Solutions could leverage their expertise to reach new markets more effectively. This partnership approach allowed for quicker entry into various regions, particularly underserved areas that could benefit from solar energy.

2. **Direct-to-Consumer Sales Model:** To enhance customer engagement and streamline the purchasing process, Solar Solutions introduced a direct-to-consumer sales model. This approach involved creating an online platform where customers could easily order solar panels and related products. By eliminating intermediaries, the company could offer competitive pricing and improve customer service.

3. **Regional Distribution Centers:** To facilitate timely deliveries and reduce shipping costs, Solar Solutions established regional distribution centers. These centers acted as hubs for inventory management and order fulfillment, allowing for faster response times to customer demands. By strategically placing these centers in key geographic locations, the company optimized its logistics operations.

4. **Utilizing Renewable Energy in Logistics:** In line with their mission, Solar Solutions made a conscious effort to incorporate renewable energy into their logistics operations. This included using electric vehicles for transportation and installing solar panels at distribution centers to power operations. This not only reduced carbon emissions but also served as a marketing point, showcasing the company's commitment to sustainability.

Challenges in Expansion

Despite the strategic initiatives, expanding production and distribution networks was not without its challenges:

1. **Supply Chain Disruptions:** The global supply chain for solar materials faced disruptions due to geopolitical tensions and natural disasters. These disruptions affected the availability of critical components, leading to delays in production. Kwame's team had to develop contingency plans and diversify suppliers to mitigate these risks.

2. **Regulatory Hurdles:** Navigating the complex regulatory landscape for renewable energy was another significant challenge. Different regions had varying regulations regarding solar installations, which complicated the distribution process. Kwame invested time in understanding these regulations and worked closely with legal experts to ensure compliance.

3. **Market Competition:** As the solar market grew, competition intensified. Other companies began to emerge with similar products, often at lower prices. To remain competitive, Solar Solutions focused on differentiating their offerings through superior technology, customer service, and community engagement initiatives.

4. **Consumer Education:** Educating consumers about the benefits of solar energy and the specifics of Solar Solutions' products was essential. Many potential customers were hesitant due to misconceptions about solar

technology. The company implemented outreach programs, workshops, and informational campaigns to address these concerns and promote awareness.

Conclusion

The expansion of production and distribution networks was a pivotal element in the success of Kwame Martins's Solar Solutions. By embracing automation, lean manufacturing, and strategic partnerships, the company was able to scale operations effectively. Despite the challenges faced, the commitment to sustainability and innovation positioned Solar Solutions as a leader in the renewable energy industry. This growth not only met the increasing demand for solar energy but also contributed to a broader movement towards a sustainable future.

Forming strategic partnerships with industry leaders

As Kwame Martins sought to scale Solar Solutions, he understood that forming strategic partnerships with industry leaders was crucial for the success and sustainability of his vision for renewable energy. These partnerships not only provided essential resources and expertise but also facilitated market access and enhanced credibility within the renewable energy sector.

The Importance of Strategic Partnerships

Strategic partnerships can be defined as alliances formed between two or more organizations that leverage each other's strengths to achieve shared goals. In the context of renewable energy, such collaborations can significantly enhance innovation, reduce costs, and accelerate the deployment of new technologies. According to the Resource-Based View (RBV) theory, firms can gain competitive advantage by acquiring valuable, rare, inimitable, and non-substitutable resources from their partners [?].

Identifying Potential Partners

Kwame recognized that not all partnerships are created equal. He focused on identifying potential partners that aligned with Solar Solutions' mission and values. Key criteria for selection included:

- **Complementary Expertise:** Partners with technical know-how in solar technology, manufacturing, or distribution could provide insights that would enhance product offerings.

+ **Market Reach:** Collaborating with established companies that had a strong market presence would allow Solar Solutions to penetrate new markets more effectively.

+ **Shared Vision:** Partnerships based on a mutual commitment to sustainability and innovation would foster a collaborative environment conducive to growth.

Examples of Strategic Partnerships

One of the first significant partnerships Kwame formed was with a leading solar panel manufacturer, SunTech Innovations. This collaboration allowed Solar Solutions to access advanced manufacturing technologies, thereby reducing production costs and increasing the efficiency of their solar panels. The partnership also enabled joint research initiatives that led to breakthroughs in photovoltaic materials, enhancing the energy conversion efficiency of their products.

Another notable partnership was established with GreenTech Finance, a financial services firm specializing in funding renewable energy projects. This partnership provided Solar Solutions with crucial financial backing to expand their operations and invest in research and development. By leveraging GreenTech's expertise in securing grants and incentives, Kwame was able to navigate the complex landscape of renewable energy financing, which is often fraught with challenges such as fluctuating government policies and market volatility.

Challenges in Forming Partnerships

Despite the advantages of strategic partnerships, Kwame faced several challenges in establishing these alliances. One significant hurdle was the skepticism from potential partners who were accustomed to traditional energy practices. Many industry leaders were hesitant to invest in solar technology, viewing it as a niche market with uncertain returns.

To address these concerns, Kwame employed a data-driven approach, presenting compelling evidence of the growing demand for renewable energy solutions. He highlighted market trends, such as the increasing cost-effectiveness of solar technology and the rising public support for clean energy, to persuade potential partners of the viability of investing in Solar Solutions.

Additionally, navigating the complexities of partnership agreements posed another challenge. Kwame had to ensure that the terms of collaboration were mutually beneficial, addressing concerns such as intellectual property rights, profit-sharing, and operational responsibilities. This required careful negotiation and, at times, compromise to foster a spirit of collaboration rather than competition.

The Impact of Strategic Partnerships on Growth

The strategic partnerships formed by Kwame Martins had a profound impact on the growth of Solar Solutions. By leveraging the resources and expertise of industry leaders, the company was able to:

+ **Accelerate Product Development:** Collaborative research initiatives led to the rapid development of innovative solar technologies that outperformed competitors.

+ **Expand Market Presence:** Partnerships with established companies facilitated entry into new markets, significantly increasing sales and brand recognition.

+ **Enhance Credibility:** Association with reputable industry leaders bolstered Solar Solutions' credibility, making it easier to attract customers and investors alike.

In conclusion, forming strategic partnerships with industry leaders was a pivotal strategy for Kwame Martins and Solar Solutions. These alliances not only provided essential resources and market access but also helped to overcome the inherent challenges of the renewable energy sector. By fostering collaboration and leveraging shared expertise, Kwame was able to drive innovation and propel Solar Solutions toward a sustainable future.

Establishing research and development facilities

In the pursuit of scaling up Solar Solutions, Kwame Martins recognized that establishing dedicated research and development (R&D) facilities was paramount to fostering innovation and ensuring the long-term viability of his solar energy initiatives. These facilities would serve as incubators for new ideas, technologies, and methodologies, allowing for the continuous improvement of solar panel efficiency and affordability.

The Importance of R&D Facilities

Research and development facilities are critical for several reasons:

+ **Innovation Catalyst:** R&D facilities provide a structured environment for scientists and engineers to experiment with new materials, designs, and technologies. This is particularly crucial in the renewable energy sector, where advancements can lead to significant breakthroughs in efficiency and cost reduction.

+ **Collaboration Hub:** These facilities foster collaboration among interdisciplinary teams, including physicists, chemists, engineers, and environmental scientists. Such collaboration can lead to innovative solutions that might not emerge in siloed environments.

+ **Attracting Talent:** A well-equipped R&D facility can attract top talent from universities and industry, eager to work on cutting-edge technologies in renewable energy. This influx of skilled professionals can accelerate the pace of innovation.

+ **Testing and Prototyping:** R&D facilities enable the testing of prototypes under controlled conditions. This is essential for validating new technologies before they are brought to market, ensuring reliability and performance.

Key Components of an Effective R&D Facility

To establish a successful R&D facility, several key components must be considered:

+ **State-of-the-Art Equipment:** Investment in advanced laboratory equipment, such as solar simulators, spectrometers, and fabrication tools, is essential. These tools facilitate the research and development of high-efficiency solar panels and innovative energy storage solutions.

+ **Sustainable Infrastructure:** The facility itself should exemplify the principles of sustainability. This includes utilizing renewable energy sources for its operations, implementing energy-efficient systems, and incorporating green building materials. Such practices not only reduce operational costs but also serve as a model for the industry.

+ **Funding and Resources:** Securing funding for R&D is crucial. This can come from various sources, including government grants, private investments, and partnerships with academic institutions. A well-funded R&D facility can pursue ambitious projects that push the boundaries of solar technology.

- **Intellectual Property Management:** Establishing a robust framework for managing intellectual property (IP) is vital. This includes protecting patents for new inventions and ensuring that the innovations developed within the facility can be commercialized effectively.

Addressing Challenges in R&D

While the establishment of R&D facilities presents numerous opportunities, it also comes with challenges:

- **High Initial Investment:** The initial costs of setting up R&D facilities can be substantial. This includes expenditures on equipment, infrastructure, and staffing. Kwame had to navigate these financial hurdles, often seeking partnerships and sponsorships to alleviate the burden.

- **Regulatory Hurdles:** Compliance with environmental regulations and safety standards can complicate the establishment of R&D facilities. Kwame's team had to work closely with regulatory bodies to ensure that their operations met all necessary guidelines.

- **Maintaining Focus:** As R&D facilities often explore a range of projects, maintaining focus on core objectives can be challenging. Kwame implemented strategic planning sessions to ensure that the team's efforts aligned with the overarching mission of Solar Solutions.

Case Study: The Solar Innovation Lab

To illustrate the impact of R&D facilities, consider the establishment of the Solar Innovation Lab (SIL) under Kwame's leadership. This facility was designed to focus on three primary areas: enhancing solar cell efficiency, developing energy storage solutions, and creating sustainable manufacturing processes.

Enhancing Solar Cell Efficiency   One of the primary goals of SIL was to improve the efficiency of photovoltaic cells. Through rigorous testing and experimentation, the team developed a new type of solar cell using perovskite materials, which demonstrated a significant increase in conversion efficiency compared to traditional silicon-based cells. The equation for efficiency (η) can be expressed as:

$$\eta = \frac{P_{\text{out}}}{P_{\text{in}}} \times 100\% \tag{24}$$

where P_{out} is the electrical power output and P_{in} is the incident solar power. The SIL's innovations led to cells achieving efficiencies exceeding 25%, a remarkable feat in the industry.

Developing Energy Storage Solutions Recognizing the importance of energy storage for solar energy viability, SIL also focused on developing advanced battery technologies. The team explored lithium-sulfur batteries, which offer higher energy density compared to conventional lithium-ion batteries. The energy density (E_d) can be defined as:

$$E_d = \frac{E_{stored}}{V} \tag{25}$$

where E_{stored} is the stored energy and V is the volume of the battery. The innovations at SIL resulted in prototypes that could store more energy in less space, making solar energy more reliable and accessible.

Creating Sustainable Manufacturing Processes SIL also prioritized sustainability in manufacturing processes. By implementing a closed-loop system, the facility minimized waste and reduced the environmental impact of solar panel production. This approach not only aligned with Kwame's vision but also set a precedent for the industry, demonstrating that sustainability and profitability can go hand in hand.

Conclusion

In summary, establishing research and development facilities is a critical step in advancing the goals of Solar Solutions. These facilities not only promote innovation and collaboration but also address the pressing challenges associated with renewable energy technologies. Through strategic investments, a focus on sustainability, and a commitment to excellence, Kwame Martins's R&D initiatives have positioned Solar Solutions at the forefront of the green energy movement, paving the way for a brighter, more sustainable future.

Empowering communities with solar energy

Bringing electricity to rural and underserved areas

Access to electricity remains a significant challenge in many rural and underserved areas around the globe. According to the International Energy Agency (IEA), approximately 770 million people still lack access to electricity, with a disproportionate number residing in remote locations. This lack of access not only hampers economic development but also affects health, education, and overall quality of life. In this context, Kwame Martins's Solar Solutions aims to bridge this gap by providing sustainable and affordable solar energy options to these communities.

The Importance of Electrification

Electrification is a catalyst for socio-economic development. It enables essential services such as healthcare, education, and clean water access. Furthermore, it fosters local entrepreneurship by allowing businesses to operate more efficiently. For instance, a study by the World Bank found that rural electrification can increase household income by up to 30%, providing families with the means to invest in education and health.

Challenges in Electrification

Despite the clear benefits of electrification, several challenges persist:

* **Infrastructure Limitations:** Many rural areas lack the necessary infrastructure for traditional grid connections. The cost of extending power lines to remote locations can be prohibitive.

* **Financial Barriers:** Low-income households often cannot afford the upfront costs associated with solar installations, despite the long-term savings on energy bills.

* **Awareness and Education:** There is often a lack of understanding about solar technology and its benefits, which can lead to skepticism and resistance to adopting new solutions.

* **Maintenance and Reliability:** Ensuring that solar systems are maintained and operational in remote areas can pose logistical challenges, especially where technical expertise is scarce.

Solar Solutions' Approach

Kwame Martins's Solar Solutions addresses these challenges through a multi-faceted approach:

where P_i represents the power output of each solar panel installed, and n is the number of panels.

The project resulted in a 50% reduction in reliance on kerosene lamps, leading to significant cost savings for families. Additionally, the local school reported a 40% increase in student attendance due to improved lighting for evening study sessions. Health clinics benefited from the ability to store vaccines and provide better care during nighttime hours.

Conclusion

Bringing electricity to rural and underserved areas is a crucial step towards achieving global energy equity. Through innovative solutions, community engagement, and strategic partnerships, Kwame Martins's Solar Solutions is making significant strides in addressing this challenge. By harnessing the power of solar energy, these initiatives not only provide access to electricity but also empower communities, stimulate economic growth, and improve overall quality of life. The journey towards sustainable electrification is ongoing, but with continued efforts and innovations, a brighter future powered by renewable energy is within reach for all.

Creating job opportunities and economic growth

The transition to solar energy not only addresses the pressing need for sustainable power sources but also serves as a catalyst for economic development. By establishing Solar Solutions, Kwame Martins has not only pioneered advancements in renewable energy technology but has also created a plethora of job opportunities that stimulate local economies. This section explores the mechanisms through which solar energy initiatives generate employment and foster economic growth, supported by relevant theories and real-world examples.

Job Creation Mechanisms

The job creation potential of the solar energy sector can be understood through several key mechanisms:

+ **Manufacturing and Installation:** The production of solar panels requires a skilled workforce. Manufacturing jobs are created in factories that produce photovoltaic cells, panels, and related components. Installation jobs emerge as more households and businesses adopt solar technology. According to the Solar Foundation's National Solar Jobs Census, the U.S. solar industry employed over 250,000 workers in 2019, showcasing significant job growth over the previous decade.

+ **Maintenance and Support Services:** Once solar systems are installed, they require regular maintenance and support. This creates opportunities for technicians and engineers who specialize in solar technology. The Bureau of Labor Statistics projects that jobs for solar photovoltaic installers will grow by 63% from 2018 to 2028, much faster than the average for all occupations.

+ **Research and Development (R&D):** The continuous evolution of solar technology necessitates ongoing research and development. This sector requires scientists, engineers, and researchers, contributing to innovation and technological advancement. By investing in R&D, Solar Solutions not only enhances its product offerings but also creates high-skilled jobs that drive economic growth.

Economic Growth Theories

The impact of job creation in the solar sector can be analyzed through various economic theories:

+ **Multiplier Effect:** The multiplier effect posits that an initial increase in spending (in this case, investment in solar energy) leads to increased income and consumption in the economy. For instance, when Solar Solutions hires local workers, these employees spend their earnings on goods and services, further stimulating the economy. The multiplier effect can be quantified using the formula:

$$\text{Total Economic Impact} = \text{Initial Investment} \times \text{Multiplier} \quad (27)$$

If Solar Solutions invests $1 million and the local multiplier is estimated at 1.5, the total economic impact million.

+ **Human Capital Theory:** This theory emphasizes the value of investing in education and training to enhance workforce skills. As Kwame's initiatives provide training programs for solar technology, they improve the skill set of local workers, leading to higher productivity and wages. This investment in human capital not only benefits individuals but also contributes to overall economic growth.

+ **Sustainable Development:** The concept of sustainable development encompasses economic growth that meets the needs of the present without compromising future generations. By focusing on renewable energy, Kwame Martins aligns with the United Nations Sustainable Development Goals (SDGs), particularly Goal 8, which promotes sustained, inclusive, and sustainable economic growth, full and productive employment, and decent work for all.

Real-World Examples

Numerous case studies illustrate the positive impact of solar energy initiatives on job creation and economic growth:

+ **California's Solar Industry:** California is a leader in solar energy adoption, with over 1 million solar installations as of 2020. The state's solar sector has created hundreds of thousands of jobs, ranging from manufacturing to installation and maintenance. The California Solar Initiative, launched in 2007, has played a crucial role in incentivizing solar adoption and driving job growth.

+ **Germany's Energiewende:** Germany's ambitious energy transition, known as Energiewende, has significantly expanded its renewable energy sector. As a result, Germany has created over 300,000 jobs in the solar industry. The government's commitment to renewable energy has not only reduced carbon emissions but has also stimulated economic growth through job creation and technological innovation.

+ **Community Solar Projects:** Community solar projects, which allow multiple households to share the benefits of a single solar installation, have emerged as a viable solution for expanding access to solar energy. These projects create local jobs in installation, maintenance, and management while providing affordable energy options for participants. An example includes the Solar Gardens program in Minnesota, which has fostered local job growth and empowered communities.

Conclusion

Creating job opportunities and fostering economic growth are integral components of Kwame Martins's vision for Solar Solutions. By investing in renewable energy, not only does Kwame contribute to a sustainable future, but he also uplifts local economies and empowers individuals through meaningful employment. The solar industry's potential for job creation is vast, and as more communities embrace clean energy solutions, the economic benefits will continue to expand, paving the way for a greener and more prosperous future.

Implementing sustainable development projects

Sustainable development projects are essential for ensuring that the benefits of renewable energy, particularly solar energy, extend beyond mere energy production. These projects aim to create a holistic approach to community development that encompasses economic, social, and environmental dimensions. In this section, we will explore the theoretical frameworks behind sustainable development, the challenges faced during implementation, and real-world examples of successful initiatives.

Theoretical Frameworks

Sustainable development is often defined through the lens of the Brundtland Report, which states that it is "development that meets the needs of the present without compromising the ability of future generations to meet their own needs" [?]. This definition emphasizes the interconnection between economic growth, environmental stewardship, and social equity.

The three pillars of sustainable development—economic viability, social inclusion, and environmental protection—are critical in shaping projects that utilize solar energy. For instance, the **Triple Bottom Line** (TBL) framework, which evaluates projects based on their social, environmental, and economic impacts, can be applied to assess the effectiveness of solar initiatives. The equation for TBL can be expressed as:

$$TBL = \text{Social Impact} + \text{Environmental Impact} + \text{Economic Impact} \quad (28)$$

This holistic approach helps ensure that solar projects do not merely focus on energy production but also contribute positively to the communities they serve.

Challenges in Implementation

Implementing sustainable development projects poses several challenges, including:

+ **Financial Constraints:** Many communities, especially in rural or underserved areas, lack the financial resources to invest in solar technology. Initial costs for solar panels and associated infrastructure can be prohibitively high.

+ **Regulatory Hurdles:** Navigating local and national regulations can be complex. Policies may not be conducive to renewable energy projects, leading to delays or cancellations.

+ **Community Engagement:** Successful implementation requires the active participation of community members. Resistance to change or lack of understanding of solar technology can hinder project adoption.

+ **Technical Challenges:** Issues such as energy storage, integration with existing grids, and maintenance of solar systems can pose significant obstacles.

Examples of Successful Projects

Despite these challenges, there are numerous successful examples of sustainable development projects that have effectively integrated solar energy into community development.

1. Solar Water Pumping in Rural India In rural India, the Solar Water Pumping project has transformed agricultural practices by providing farmers with reliable access to water. Traditional pumping methods often relied on fossil fuels, which were both expensive and environmentally damaging. By implementing solar-powered pumps, farmers can irrigate their fields sustainably.

The project not only improves crop yields but also reduces dependency on non-renewable resources, thereby promoting environmental sustainability. The economic impact is significant, with farmers reporting a reduction in water costs by up to 50% [?].

2. Solar Microgrids in Africa In several African countries, solar microgrid projects have been established to provide electricity to off-grid communities. These microgrids are designed to be community-owned and managed, ensuring that the benefits of solar energy are shared among local residents.

For example, the project in rural Kenya has empowered communities by providing access to electricity for schools, health clinics, and businesses. The economic growth resulting from reliable electricity has been profound, with local businesses reporting a 30% increase in revenue [?].

3. Solar-Powered Schools in the Philippines   In the Philippines, a project aimed at installing solar panels in schools has not only provided reliable electricity but also served as a platform for education about renewable energy. Students learn about solar technology and its benefits, fostering a culture of sustainability from a young age.

This initiative has led to improved educational outcomes, as schools can now offer extended hours and utilize technology that was previously unavailable. Furthermore, the project has created jobs for local technicians, thereby addressing both educational and economic needs [?].

Conclusion

Implementing sustainable development projects that leverage solar energy is vital for fostering community resilience and promoting long-term environmental sustainability. By addressing financial, regulatory, and technical challenges, and by drawing on successful examples from around the globe, innovators like Kwame Martins can create impactful solutions that empower communities and contribute to a greener future. The integration of solar energy into sustainable development not only addresses the immediate energy needs of communities but also lays the groundwork for a more sustainable and equitable world.

Chapter Four: Influencing Policy and Public Opinion

Advocacy for renewable energy policies

Lobbying for government support and incentives

As Kwame Martins sought to revolutionize the renewable energy landscape with his company, Solar Solutions, he recognized that one of the most significant barriers to the widespread adoption of solar energy was the lack of supportive government policies and incentives. This realization marked a pivotal moment in his journey as he began to engage in lobbying efforts aimed at influencing governmental support for renewable energy initiatives.

Understanding the Importance of Government Support

Government support can take various forms, including financial incentives, tax credits, grants, and subsidies that lower the cost of solar energy production and installation. According to the *International Energy Agency (IEA)*, effective government policies can lead to a substantial increase in the adoption of renewable energy technologies. For instance, the introduction of the **Investment Tax Credit (ITC)** in the United States has been credited with boosting solar installations by over 1,600% since its inception in 2006.

The mathematical representation of the impact of such incentives can be described using the following equation:

$$E = C \cdot (1 - T) \tag{29}$$

Where:

+ E is the effective cost of solar energy installation,

- C is the original cost of installation,

- T is the tax incentive as a decimal (e.g., a 30% tax credit would be $T = 0.30$).

This equation illustrates how tax incentives directly reduce the financial burden on consumers and businesses, thereby promoting the adoption of solar technology.

Identifying Key Stakeholders

Kwame understood that successful lobbying requires identifying and engaging key stakeholders, including policymakers, government officials, and industry leaders. Building relationships with these individuals was crucial in advocating for policies that favor renewable energy. He organized meetings, participated in industry conferences, and collaborated with environmental organizations to amplify his voice.

One notable example of effective lobbying was Kwame's collaboration with the **National Renewable Energy Laboratory** (**NREL**). By presenting research and data demonstrating the economic benefits of solar energy—such as job creation and reduced energy costs—Kwame was able to persuade several legislators to consider introducing more favorable policies for solar energy.

Challenges in the Lobbying Process

Despite his efforts, Kwame faced numerous challenges in the lobbying process. One significant problem was the entrenched interests of traditional energy companies, which often lobbied against renewable energy initiatives. These companies had substantial financial resources and political influence, making it difficult for new entrants like Solar Solutions to compete on equal footing.

Moreover, the complexity of the legislative process posed another hurdle. Understanding the nuances of energy policy, regulatory frameworks, and the political landscape was essential for effective lobbying. Kwame often relied on experts in public policy and law to help navigate these challenges.

Strategies for Effective Lobbying

To overcome these obstacles, Kwame employed several strategies:

- **Data-Driven Advocacy:** By presenting clear, empirical data on the benefits of solar energy, Kwame was able to make a compelling case for government support. He utilized statistics showing how solar energy could reduce greenhouse gas emissions by $\sim$ 1.5 billion metric tons annually if fully adopted.

+ **Grassroots Mobilization:** Kwame encouraged community members and solar energy advocates to voice their support for renewable energy policies. This grassroots approach not only amplified the message but also demonstrated to lawmakers that there was significant public interest in transitioning to renewable energy sources.

+ **Coalition Building:** Forming coalitions with other renewable energy companies and environmental organizations helped to consolidate resources and strengthen lobbying efforts. By presenting a united front, they were able to exert greater influence on policymakers.

Case Studies of Successful Lobbying Efforts

Several successful lobbying efforts across the globe serve as inspiration for Kwame's initiatives. For example, in Germany, the **Renewable Energy Sources Act (EEG)** was enacted in 2000, establishing a feed-in tariff system that guaranteed fixed payments for renewable energy producers. This policy has led to Germany becoming a leader in solar energy production, with over 45 gigawatts of installed solar capacity by 2021.

Similarly, in Australia, the **Small-scale Renewable Energy Scheme (SRES)** provides incentives for households and small businesses to install solar panels, resulting in a significant increase in solar adoption. These examples demonstrate the power of effective lobbying in shaping energy policy and promoting renewable energy technologies.

Conclusion

In summary, Kwame Martins's lobbying for government support and incentives was a critical aspect of his journey as a green energy pioneer. By understanding the importance of government policies, identifying key stakeholders, overcoming challenges, and employing effective strategies, he was able to advocate for a sustainable future powered by solar energy. The ongoing efforts to influence policy will continue to play a crucial role in the transition towards a cleaner, greener planet.

Educating policymakers on the benefits of solar energy

In the quest for a sustainable future, one of the pivotal roles played by Kwame Martins and his organization, Solar Solutions, has been the education of policymakers regarding the myriad benefits of solar energy. This endeavor is not merely about presenting facts; it encompasses a comprehensive strategy to shift perceptions, influence legislative actions, and foster an environment conducive to renewable energy adoption.

The Importance of Education

The foundation of effective policymaking lies in a well-informed decision-making process. Policymakers often rely on data, research, and expert opinions to guide their legislative initiatives. Therefore, educating them on solar energy's benefits is crucial for several reasons:

+ **Economic Advantages:** Solar energy has become increasingly cost-effective. According to the International Renewable Energy Agency (IRENA), the cost of solar photovoltaic (PV) systems has dropped by over 80% since 2010. This reduction can be illustrated with the following equation:

$$\text{Cost}_{2020} = \text{Cost}_{2010} \times (1 - \text{Rate of Decline})^{\text{Years}} \qquad (30)$$

where the Rate of Decline is approximately 0.2 for an 80% decrease over 10 years. Presenting these statistics to policymakers can help them understand the economic viability of solar energy as a sustainable alternative.

+ **Job Creation:** The solar industry has proven to be a significant job creator. As reported by the Solar Foundation's National Solar Jobs Census, the U.S. solar industry employed over 250,000 workers in 2019, a number that continues to grow. This point can be emphasized through case studies of successful solar projects that have generated local employment, showcasing how investment in solar can stimulate economic growth in various regions.

+ **Environmental Impact:** Solar energy offers a clean alternative to fossil fuels, significantly reducing greenhouse gas emissions. According to the U.S. Environmental Protection Agency (EPA), solar energy systems can reduce carbon emissions by as much as 80% compared to traditional energy sources. Educating policymakers about the positive environmental impact of solar energy can encourage them to support legislation aimed at reducing carbon footprints.

Strategies for Educating Policymakers

To effectively educate policymakers, Kwame Martins and his team employed several strategies:

+ **Workshops and Seminars:** Organizing workshops and seminars that bring together experts in the field of renewable energy to share insights and data with policymakers. These events provide a platform for interactive discussions and allow policymakers to ask questions directly.

+ **Data-Driven Reports:** Producing comprehensive reports that compile data on the economic, environmental, and social benefits of solar energy. These reports often include infographics and case studies to make the information accessible and engaging. For instance, a report might illustrate the correlation between solar energy adoption and job growth in a particular state.

+ **Collaborations with Research Institutions:** Partnering with universities and research institutions to conduct studies that provide empirical evidence on the benefits of solar energy. Such collaborations lend credibility to the information presented to policymakers.

+ **Direct Engagement:** Establishing direct lines of communication with policymakers through meetings, phone calls, and emails to discuss the benefits of solar energy. Personal stories and testimonials from communities that have benefited from solar energy can be particularly persuasive.

Challenges in Educating Policymakers

Despite the efforts made, several challenges persist in educating policymakers about solar energy:

+ **Resistance to Change:** Many policymakers have longstanding ties to traditional energy industries, which can create resistance to adopting new energy solutions. Overcoming this resistance requires persistent advocacy and the demonstration of solar energy's viability.

+ **Misinformation:** The presence of misinformation regarding solar energy—whether about its efficiency, cost, or practicality—can hinder progress. Addressing these misconceptions through clear, factual communication is essential.

+ **Short-Term Focus:** Policymakers often prioritize immediate economic concerns over long-term sustainability goals. Emphasizing the long-term financial benefits of solar energy, such as reduced energy costs and energy independence, can help shift this perspective.

Examples of Successful Education Initiatives

Several initiatives led by Solar Solutions have successfully educated policymakers on the benefits of solar energy:

+ **The Green Energy Summit:** An annual event where leaders in renewable energy, including Kwame Martins, present their findings to local and national policymakers. This summit has resulted in the introduction of several renewable energy bills aimed at increasing solar adoption.

+ **Community Outreach Programs:** Engaging local communities to share their experiences with solar energy, which in turn influences local policymakers. For example, a community in a rural area that transitioned to solar power showcased significant cost savings, prompting local government to consider solar incentives.

In conclusion, educating policymakers on the benefits of solar energy is a critical component of advancing the renewable energy agenda. By employing strategic approaches, overcoming challenges, and showcasing successful initiatives, Kwame Martins and Solar Solutions continue to pave the way for a sustainable energy future, ensuring that the voices of innovation and environmental stewardship resonate within the halls of power.

Promoting renewable energy legislation

Promoting renewable energy legislation is a critical aspect of Kwame Martins's mission to advance solar energy solutions and combat the global energy crisis. The legislative framework surrounding renewable energy not only shapes the market dynamics but also influences public perception and investment in clean technologies. This section delves into the strategies employed by Kwame and his team to advocate for policies that support renewable energy development, the challenges they faced, and the successes they achieved.

The Importance of Legislative Support

Renewable energy legislation encompasses a wide range of policies, incentives, and regulations designed to promote the development and integration of renewable energy sources into the energy grid. These policies can include tax credits, subsidies, renewable portfolio standards (RPS), and feed-in tariffs. The significance of legislative support for renewable energy is underscored by the following key points:

+ **Financial Incentives:** Legislation that offers tax credits or rebates can significantly reduce the upfront costs associated with solar installations, making them more accessible to consumers and businesses. For instance, the federal Investment Tax Credit (ITC) allows homeowners and businesses to deduct a percentage of the cost of installing a solar energy system from their federal taxes.

+ **Market Stability:** Clear and consistent renewable energy policies provide a stable environment for investors. This stability encourages private sector investment, which is crucial for scaling up solar technologies. A study by the International Renewable Energy Agency (IRENA) indicated that countries with robust renewable energy legislation attracted significantly more investments compared to those without.

+ **Long-term Planning:** Effective legislation facilitates long-term planning for energy infrastructure, enabling utilities and businesses to integrate renewable sources into their energy mix. This is essential for meeting growing energy demands while reducing greenhouse gas emissions.

Challenges in Promoting Legislation

Despite the clear benefits of renewable energy legislation, Kwame faced several challenges in advocating for these policies. These challenges included:

+ **Political Resistance:** Many politicians and stakeholders in the fossil fuel industry resisted renewable energy legislation due to economic interests and political affiliations. Kwame often encountered pushback from lobbyists representing traditional energy sectors, who argued against the viability of solar energy as a primary energy source.

+ **Public Misconceptions:** Public understanding of renewable energy technologies was often limited. Misconceptions about the efficiency and reliability of solar energy systems hindered legislative progress. To combat this, Kwame and his team focused on educational campaigns to inform the public about the benefits of solar energy.

+ **Complex Regulatory Frameworks:** Navigating the intricate web of federal, state, and local regulations posed a significant challenge. Different jurisdictions had varying policies, which complicated the promotion of a unified renewable energy agenda.

Strategies for Advocacy

To overcome these challenges, Kwame employed several strategies to promote renewable energy legislation effectively:

+ **Building Coalitions:** Kwame recognized the power of collaboration. He formed coalitions with other renewable energy advocates, environmental organizations, and community groups. By uniting diverse stakeholders, they amplified their voice and increased their influence on policymakers.

+ **Engaging with Policymakers:** Kwame actively engaged with lawmakers at all levels of government. He organized meetings, attended hearings, and provided expert testimony on the benefits of renewable energy. By establishing himself as a credible source of information, he was able to sway opinions and garner support for key legislation.

+ **Utilizing Data and Research:** To strengthen his arguments, Kwame relied on empirical data and research findings. He presented studies showing the economic benefits of renewable energy, such as job creation and reduced energy costs. For example, a report from the Solar Foundation highlighted that the solar industry employed over 250,000 workers in the United States alone, demonstrating the sector's potential for economic growth.

+ **Grassroots Mobilization:** Kwame understood the importance of grassroots movements in influencing policy. He encouraged community members to voice their support for renewable energy legislation through petitions, public demonstrations, and social media campaigns. This grassroots pressure often prompted lawmakers to take action.

Case Studies of Successful Legislation

Kwame's advocacy efforts contributed to several successful legislative initiatives that advanced renewable energy adoption:

- **California's SB 100:** In 2018, California passed Senate Bill 100, which mandates that the state transition to 100% clean energy by 2045. This ambitious legislation was the result of years of advocacy from renewable energy proponents, including Kwame's coalition.

- **The Green New Deal:** While still a proposal, the Green New Deal sparked significant national dialogue about renewable energy and climate change. Kwame's involvement in promoting the principles of the Green New Deal helped elevate the conversation around renewable energy legislation in Congress.

- **Local Initiatives:** Many cities and states adopted their own renewable energy targets and incentives. Kwame's team worked with local governments to implement programs that encouraged solar installations, such as streamlined permitting processes and community solar projects.

Conclusion

Promoting renewable energy legislation is an essential component of Kwame Martins's vision for a sustainable future. Through strategic advocacy, coalition-building, and public engagement, he has played a pivotal role in shaping policies that support the growth of solar energy. As the world continues to grapple with the challenges of climate change and energy sustainability, Kwame's efforts serve as a testament to the power of legislation in driving the transition towards a cleaner, greener future.

Media and public outreach

Leveraging social media and digital platforms

In the contemporary landscape of communication, social media and digital platforms have become essential tools for advocacy and public outreach, particularly in the realm of renewable energy. For Kwame Martins and his initiative, Solar Solutions, these platforms provide a unique opportunity to engage with diverse audiences, disseminate information, and mobilize support for solar energy initiatives.

Theoretical Framework

The use of social media in advocacy can be understood through the lens of the *Diffusion of Innovations Theory*, which posits that new ideas and technologies spread through specific channels over time among members of a social system. According to Rogers (2003), the process involves several stages: knowledge, persuasion, decision, implementation, and confirmation. Social media serves as a powerful channel for the first two stages—knowledge and persuasion—by facilitating rapid dissemination of information and enabling interaction with potential adopters.

Challenges in the Digital Space

While the potential of social media is immense, several challenges persist:

+ **Misinformation:** The rapid spread of false information can undermine legitimate efforts. For instance, misconceptions about solar energy's efficiency or costs can deter potential users. A study by Lewandowsky et al. (2012) highlights how misinformation can persist even after corrections are made, complicating public understanding.

+ **Engagement Fatigue:** With the sheer volume of content available online, users may experience engagement fatigue, leading to diminished attention spans and reduced interaction with advocacy messages. This phenomenon requires innovative strategies to capture and maintain audience interest.

+ **Algorithmic Bias:** Social media platforms often use algorithms that prioritize certain types of content over others, which can create echo chambers. This bias can limit the reach of messages promoting renewable energy, as they may not be presented to users who do not already engage with similar content.

Strategies for Effective Engagement

To overcome these challenges and effectively leverage social media, Kwame Martins employed several strategies:

+ **Content Creation:** Engaging, informative, and visually appealing content is crucial. For example, Solar Solutions created infographics that illustrated the benefits of solar energy, making complex information accessible to a broader audience.

gained access to electricity through solar power, emphasizing the transformative potential of renewable energy.

To support his arguments, Kwame incorporated relevant statistics and research findings. For instance, he would cite the International Renewable Energy Agency's (IRENA) report indicating that solar energy could provide up to 30% of the world's energy needs by 2030. He presented equations that illustrated the efficiency of solar panels over time, such as:

$$E = P \times t$$

where E is the energy produced, P is the power output of the solar panel, and t is the time of sunlight exposure. This mathematical representation helped to ground his arguments in scientific reality.

Engaging the Audience

Kwame was adept at engaging his audience through interactive presentations. He often used visual aids, such as infographics and videos, to demonstrate the impact of solar energy on reducing carbon footprints. For example, he would show a graph comparing the carbon emissions of fossil fuels versus solar energy over a decade, highlighting the stark difference:

$$CO_2 \text{ emissions} = \frac{\text{Total fossil fuel consumption}}{\text{Energy produced by solar}}$$

This visual representation not only captured attention but also made the data more digestible.

Furthermore, he encouraged audience participation by posing thought-provoking questions, such as: "What would our cities look like if every rooftop was equipped with solar panels?" This technique not only fostered engagement but also prompted attendees to envision a sustainable future.

Networking and Collaboration Opportunities

Conferences also served as a networking platform for Kwame, allowing him to connect with other innovators, researchers, and policymakers. He often participated in panel discussions and workshops, where he could share insights and learn from others in the field. These interactions led to collaborations that were instrumental in advancing Solar Solutions' technology and outreach efforts.

For example, during a renewable energy summit, Kwame met with representatives from a non-profit organization focused on providing solar energy solutions to underserved communities. This connection led to a partnership that enabled Solar Solutions to expand its reach and impact.

Impact of Speaking Engagements

Kwame's speaking engagements significantly contributed to raising awareness about solar energy and its potential benefits. He often received feedback from attendees who expressed newfound interest in renewable energy initiatives. His speeches not only educated but also inspired action, leading to increased community involvement in local solar projects.

Moreover, the media coverage of his talks helped amplify his message, reaching a broader audience beyond the conference attendees. Articles highlighting his presentations often appeared in local newspapers and online platforms, further solidifying his role as a thought leader in the green energy movement.

Conclusion

In conclusion, Kwame Martins's commitment to speaking at conferences and events played a crucial role in promoting solar energy and advocating for policy changes. Through effective communication, engaging storytelling, and collaborative networking, he was able to influence public opinion and inspire a new generation of innovators to join the green energy movement. The power of public speaking in advocacy cannot be overstated; it is a vital element in the ongoing fight for a sustainable future.

Writing articles and books to spread the message

Kwame Martins understood that one of the most effective ways to advocate for solar energy and its potential to transform the energy landscape was through the written word. By writing articles and books, he aimed to educate the public, influence policymakers, and inspire future innovators. This section delves into the significance of written communication in the renewable energy movement, the challenges faced, and the strategies employed by Kwame to effectively convey his message.

The Importance of Written Communication

In the digital age, written communication remains a powerful tool for disseminating information. Articles and books serve as platforms for sharing knowledge, raising awareness, and fostering dialogue. For Kwame, writing was not merely an outlet for expression; it was a strategic approach to influence public opinion and policy. Research indicates that effective communication can significantly impact public understanding and support for renewable energy initiatives [?].

Challenges in Writing about Renewable Energy

Despite the importance of writing, Kwame faced several challenges:

- **Complexity of the Subject:** Renewable energy, particularly solar power, involves intricate scientific principles and technologies. Effectively communicating these concepts to a lay audience required simplification without losing essential details.

- **Misinformation:** The prevalence of misinformation about renewable energy posed a significant hurdle. Kwame had to ensure that his writings countered false narratives and provided accurate information.

- **Engagement:** Capturing the interest of readers in a saturated media landscape was another challenge. Kwame needed to craft compelling narratives that resonated with diverse audiences.

Strategies for Effective Writing

To overcome these challenges, Kwame employed several strategies:

1. **Simplifying Complex Concepts:** Kwame utilized analogies and relatable examples to explain complex scientific ideas. For instance, he compared solar panel functionality to a flower absorbing sunlight, making the technology more approachable for readers unfamiliar with physics.

2. **Fact-Checking and Research:** To combat misinformation, Kwame prioritized thorough research and fact-checking. He collaborated with experts in the field to ensure the accuracy of his articles and books. This commitment to factual integrity helped build trust with his audience.

3. **Storytelling:** Kwame recognized the power of storytelling in engaging readers. He shared personal anecdotes and success stories from communities that had benefited from solar energy. This narrative approach not only educated but also inspired hope and action.

Examples of Impactful Writings

Kwame's writings included articles in prominent environmental journals and a bestselling book titled *Bright Futures: The Solar Revolution*. In these works, he discussed the potential of solar energy to address the global energy crisis and highlighted case studies of successful solar initiatives worldwide.

For example, in one article, he detailed the transformation of a rural village in Africa that gained access to electricity through solar microgrids. This not only improved the quality of life for residents but also fostered local entrepreneurship, demonstrating the broader socio-economic benefits of renewable energy.

Theoretical Frameworks in Communication

Kwame's approach to writing was informed by several communication theories:

+ **The Elaboration Likelihood Model (ELM):** This theory posits that individuals process persuasive messages through two routes: the central route (deep processing) and the peripheral route (superficial processing) [?]. Kwame aimed to engage readers through the central route by providing well-researched arguments and compelling narratives.

+ **Social Cognitive Theory:** This framework emphasizes the role of observational learning in behavior change [?]. By sharing stories of individuals and communities successfully adopting solar energy, Kwame aimed to inspire readers to envision themselves as part of the renewable energy movement.

Conclusion

Through his dedication to writing articles and books, Kwame Martins effectively spread the message of solar energy and its transformative potential. By overcoming challenges and employing strategic communication techniques, he not only educated the public but also inspired action and advocacy for renewable energy. His legacy as a writer underscores the vital role of communication in the fight for a sustainable future.

Chapter Five: Legacy and Future Visions

Kwame's impact on the green energy movement

Awards and recognition for his contributions

Kwame Martins's relentless pursuit of innovation in the green energy sector has not gone unnoticed. His groundbreaking work in solar technology has garnered numerous awards and accolades, reflecting both his individual contributions and the broader impact of his initiatives on the renewable energy landscape. The recognition he has received serves not only as a testament to his vision but also as an inspiration for future innovators aiming to address the world's energy crisis.

One of the most prestigious awards Kwame received is the **Global Green Energy Innovator Award**, presented annually to individuals who have made significant advancements in the field of sustainable energy. This award recognizes Kwame's ability to transform the solar energy sector through his innovative designs and efficient solar panel prototypes. His work has led to a remarkable increase in solar panel efficiency, which is often quantified using the efficiency equation:

$$\eta = \frac{P_{out}}{P_{in}} \times 100\% \tag{31}$$

where η is the efficiency, P_{out} is the output power, and P_{in} is the input power from sunlight. Kwame's solar panels have achieved efficiencies exceeding 25%, significantly higher than the industry standard of around 15% at the time of his innovations.

In addition to the Global Green Energy Innovator Award, Kwame has also been honored with the **Environmental Leadership Award** from the World Environmental Forum. This accolade highlights his advocacy for sustainable energy policies and his efforts to educate policymakers on the benefits of transitioning to renewable energy sources. His initiatives in lobbying for government incentives have led to the implementation of several key policies that promote solar energy adoption, resulting in a measurable increase in solar installations across various regions. For instance, a study conducted by the Renewable Energy Policy Network indicated that countries implementing supportive policies saw a 35% increase in solar capacity within three years.

Furthermore, Kwame was recognized by the **National Institute of Renewable Energy** with the *Innovative Technology Award* for his development of cost-effective solar storage solutions. His work in addressing the challenge of energy storage has been pivotal, especially given the intermittent nature of solar power. The energy storage capacity can be modeled by the following equation:

$$E = P \cdot t \tag{32}$$

where E is the energy stored, P is the power rating of the storage system, and t is the duration for which the power can be stored. Kwame's innovative storage systems have allowed for greater energy reliability, making solar energy a viable option for both urban and rural communities.

Kwame's contributions extend beyond technical innovations; he has also been a strong advocate for community empowerment through renewable energy. His efforts have been recognized with the **Community Impact Award** from the Green Energy Coalition, which honors individuals whose work has made a substantial difference in underserved communities. By implementing solar projects in rural areas, Kwame has helped to provide electricity to thousands of households, creating job opportunities and fostering economic growth. The impact of these projects can be measured through indicators such as increased local employment rates and enhanced access to education and healthcare.

Moreover, Kwame has been featured in various publications and media outlets, further solidifying his status as a thought leader in the renewable energy sector. His articles and interviews often highlight the importance of interdisciplinary collaboration in tackling the energy crisis. He emphasizes that the integration of technology, policy, and community engagement is essential for creating sustainable energy solutions.

In summary, the awards and recognition Kwame Martins has received are a reflection of his significant contributions to the green energy movement. They underscore the importance of innovation, advocacy, and community involvement in achieving a sustainable energy future. Kwame's journey serves as a beacon of hope and a model for aspiring innovators, illustrating that with determination and creativity, it is possible to effect meaningful change in the world.

Inspiring the next generation of innovators

Kwame Martins's journey as a green energy pioneer serves not only as a testament to the power of innovation but also as a beacon of inspiration for the next generation of innovators. His story embodies the principles of resilience, creativity, and the relentless pursuit of a sustainable future. As he shares his experiences, he instills a belief that young minds can also contribute to solving the world's pressing energy crisis.

The Role of Education

Education plays a pivotal role in shaping future innovators. Kwame often emphasizes the importance of STEM (Science, Technology, Engineering, and Mathematics) education, advocating for increased accessibility and engagement in these fields. He believes that fostering a strong foundation in these subjects equips young individuals with the critical thinking skills necessary to tackle complex problems.

For instance, Kwame frequently collaborates with educational institutions to develop programs that introduce students to renewable energy concepts. These programs often include hands-on workshops where students can design and prototype their own solar-powered devices. By engaging students in practical applications of their learning, Kwame aims to spark their interest in green technologies.

Mentorship and Support Networks

Inspiring the next generation also requires a robust support system. Kwame often recounts the mentors who guided him during his formative years. He actively seeks to replicate this experience by establishing mentorship programs that connect aspiring innovators with industry veterans. These mentorship programs not only provide guidance but also foster a sense of community among young innovators.

A notable example of this initiative is the "Solar Innovators" program, which pairs high school students with professionals in the renewable energy sector. Participants engage in projects that allow them to explore real-world challenges, such as designing solar solutions for local communities. This hands-on experience not only enhances their technical skills but also cultivates a sense of responsibility towards societal issues.

Emphasizing Diversity and Inclusion

Kwame understands that innovation thrives in diverse environments. He actively promotes diversity and inclusion within the field of renewable energy, encouraging individuals from various backgrounds to contribute their unique perspectives. He often points out that the most groundbreaking ideas often emerge from the intersection of different cultures and experiences.

To this end, Kwame supports initiatives aimed at increasing participation from underrepresented groups in STEM fields. For example, he collaborates with organizations that provide scholarships and resources to students from marginalized communities, ensuring that financial barriers do not hinder their pursuit of careers in renewable energy.

Using Technology for Outreach

In the digital age, technology serves as a powerful tool for outreach and inspiration. Kwame leverages social media platforms and digital content to share his journey and the importance of renewable energy. Through engaging videos, podcasts, and online workshops, he reaches a global audience, inspiring young innovators to think critically about energy solutions.

One of his most impactful campaigns, "Solar Stories," invites young innovators to share their projects and ideas through social media. This initiative not only showcases their creativity but also builds a sense of belonging within the renewable energy community. By highlighting the achievements of young innovators, Kwame reinforces the idea that anyone can make a difference.

Encouraging Entrepreneurial Mindsets

Kwame believes that fostering an entrepreneurial mindset is crucial for the next generation of innovators. He encourages young people to embrace failure as a learning opportunity and to view challenges as stepping stones towards success. By sharing his own setbacks and how he overcame them, he instills resilience in aspiring innovators.

Workshops focused on entrepreneurial skills, such as business planning and funding strategies, are integral to Kwame's outreach efforts. He often invites successful entrepreneurs from the renewable energy sector to share their experiences, providing valuable insights into the journey of bringing innovative ideas to market.

Conclusion

Kwame Martins's commitment to inspiring the next generation of innovators is evident in his multifaceted approach. Through education, mentorship, diversity initiatives, technology outreach, and entrepreneurial support, he cultivates an environment where young minds can thrive. His belief in the potential of the next generation is unwavering, and he continues to champion their efforts to create a sustainable future. As Kwame often states, "The innovators of tomorrow are the architects of a brighter, greener world."

The future of Solar Solutions and the renewable energy industry

The future of Solar Solutions, under the visionary leadership of Kwame Martins, is poised to redefine not only the renewable energy landscape but also the socioeconomic fabric of communities worldwide. As we look ahead, several key themes emerge that will shape the trajectory of both Solar Solutions and the broader renewable energy industry.

Technological Advancements

One of the most significant drivers of change in the solar energy sector is technological innovation. The continuous improvement of solar panel efficiency is paramount. Current photovoltaic (PV) technology, primarily based on silicon, has reached efficiencies around 20-25%. However, emerging materials such as perovskite solar cells show promise for efficiencies exceeding 30% [?].

The equation governing the efficiency of a solar cell can be expressed as:

$$\eta = \frac{P_{out}}{P_{in}} \times 100 \tag{33}$$

where η is the efficiency, P_{out} is the electrical power output, and P_{in} is the solar power input. As new materials and technologies emerge, the industry must adapt to integrate these advancements into existing production processes.

Energy Storage Solutions

As solar energy generation is inherently intermittent, the development of effective energy storage solutions is crucial. Current battery technologies, such as lithium-ion batteries, face challenges regarding cost, lifecycle, and environmental impact. Innovations in solid-state batteries and alternative chemistries, such as sodium-ion or flow batteries, are being explored to provide scalable and sustainable storage options [?].

The relationship between energy storage capacity E, discharge time t, and power P can be described by the equation:

$$E = P \times t \tag{34}$$

This relationship highlights the importance of developing high-capacity, long-duration storage systems to ensure a reliable energy supply.

Policy and Economic Factors

The future of Solar Solutions is also intricately linked to policy frameworks and economic incentives. Governments worldwide are increasingly recognizing the need to transition to renewable energy sources. Policies such as feed-in tariffs, renewable portfolio standards, and tax incentives can significantly affect the growth of solar energy adoption [?].

Moreover, the economic viability of solar projects is often determined by the levelized cost of electricity (LCOE), defined as:

$$LCOE = \frac{I + M + E}{E_{output}} \tag{35}$$

where I is the initial investment, M is the maintenance cost, E is the operational costs, and E_{output} is the total energy produced over the system's lifetime. As technology improves and economies of scale are realized, the LCOE for solar energy is expected to decline, making it increasingly competitive with traditional fossil fuels.

Global Market Dynamics

The global shift towards renewable energy is not uniform; it varies by region based on local resources, government policies, and public perception. In developing countries, solar energy presents a unique opportunity to provide energy access to underserved populations. Initiatives like off-grid solar solutions can empower communities, reduce reliance on fossil fuels, and stimulate local economies [?].

Challenges Ahead

Despite the promising outlook, several challenges must be addressed. The solar industry faces issues such as supply chain vulnerabilities, particularly concerning raw materials like silicon and rare earth elements. Additionally, the recycling of solar panels at the end of their lifecycle is becoming an increasingly pressing concern, as the volume of decommissioned panels is projected to rise significantly in the coming decades [?].

Moreover, public perception and acceptance of solar technology can vary widely. Misinformation and skepticism about the efficacy and reliability of solar energy systems can hinder adoption. Therefore, educational outreach and transparent communication about the benefits and limitations of solar energy are essential for fostering public support.

Conclusion

In conclusion, the future of Solar Solutions and the renewable energy industry is bright but requires concerted efforts across multiple fronts. Through technological innovation, supportive policies, and community engagement, Solar Solutions can continue to lead the charge towards a sustainable energy future. Kwame Martins's vision not only aims to create a viable business but also to inspire a global movement towards clean energy, ensuring that future generations inherit a healthier planet.

The global shift towards clean energy sources

The decline of fossil fuels and the rise of solar power

The global energy landscape is undergoing a significant transformation, marked by the decline of fossil fuels and the meteoric rise of solar power. This shift is driven by a confluence of environmental, economic, and technological factors that are reshaping how we produce and consume energy.

The Decline of Fossil Fuels

Fossil fuels—comprising coal, oil, and natural gas—have long been the backbone of the world's energy supply. However, their dominance is increasingly challenged by growing concerns over climate change and environmental degradation. The burning of fossil fuels releases significant amounts of carbon dioxide (CO_2), a greenhouse gas that contributes to global warming. The Intergovernmental Panel on Climate Change (IPCC) has warned that to limit global warming to 1.5°C, we must reduce CO_2 emissions by approximately 45% from 2010 levels by 2030, and reach net-zero by 2050 [?].

In addition to environmental concerns, the economic viability of fossil fuels is being questioned. As reserves dwindle, extraction becomes more costly and complex. The price volatility associated with oil and gas markets can destabilize economies and lead to energy insecurity. For instance, the 2020 global oil price crash, exacerbated by the COVID-19 pandemic, highlighted the fragility of fossil fuel dependency [?].

The Rise of Solar Power

In contrast, solar power has emerged as a leading contender in the renewable energy sector, experiencing exponential growth over the past decade. According to the International Energy Agency (IEA), solar energy capacity increased from 40 gigawatts (GW) in 2010 to over 700 GW in 2020 [?]. This rapid expansion can be attributed to several key factors:

+ **Technological Advancements:** Innovations in photovoltaic (PV) technology have significantly increased the efficiency of solar panels. The introduction of bifacial panels, which capture sunlight on both sides, and advancements in perovskite solar cells have pushed conversion efficiencies beyond 25% [?].

+ **Decreasing Costs:** The cost of solar energy has plummeted, making it one of the most affordable sources of electricity. According to the Lazard Levelized Cost of Energy Analysis, the cost of utility-scale solar has dropped by 88% since 2009, making it cheaper than coal and natural gas in many regions [?].

+ **Government Policies and Incentives:** Many governments are implementing policies to encourage the adoption of solar energy. Tax credits, rebates, and feed-in tariffs have made solar installations more financially attractive for both individuals and businesses [?].

+ **Public Awareness and Demand:** As awareness of climate change grows, consumers are increasingly seeking sustainable energy solutions. This shift in public sentiment is driving demand for solar installations, both residential and commercial.

Challenges and Solutions

Despite its rapid growth, solar power faces challenges that must be addressed to ensure its continued rise. Key issues include:

+ **Intermittency:** Solar energy generation is dependent on sunlight, leading to variability in power supply. This intermittency can be mitigated through advancements in energy storage technologies, such as lithium-ion batteries and emerging solutions like flow batteries and pumped hydro storage. The equation for energy storage capacity can be expressed as:

$$E = P \times t \qquad (36)$$

where E is energy capacity (in kWh), P is power output (in kW), and t is time (in hours).

+ **Land Use:** Large-scale solar farms require significant land, which can lead to conflicts over land use. Innovative solutions such as agrivoltaics—combining agriculture and solar energy production—can optimize land use and increase food security while generating renewable energy [?].

+ **Recycling and Waste:** The lifecycle of solar panels raises concerns about waste and recycling. Developing efficient recycling processes and circular economy models is crucial to address these issues and minimize environmental impact [?].

Conclusion

The decline of fossil fuels and the rise of solar power represent a pivotal shift in the global energy paradigm. As we move towards a sustainable future, the importance of solar energy cannot be overstated. By harnessing the power of the sun, we can reduce our carbon footprint, enhance energy security, and create a cleaner, more resilient energy system. The transition to solar power is not just an opportunity; it is an imperative for a sustainable world.

Potential challenges and solutions for a sustainable future

The transition towards a sustainable future powered by renewable energy sources, particularly solar energy, is fraught with challenges that must be addressed to ensure a successful shift from fossil fuels. This section explores some of these potential challenges along with viable solutions, drawing upon current theories, empirical evidence, and real-world examples.

Intermittency of Solar Energy

One of the primary challenges associated with solar energy is its intermittent nature; solar power generation is contingent upon sunlight availability, which fluctuates throughout the day and is affected by weather conditions. This intermittency can lead to reliability issues in energy supply.

Solution: Energy Storage Technologies   To mitigate the effects of intermittency, advancements in energy storage technologies are crucial. Current solutions include:

+ **Batteries:** Lithium-ion batteries have become the dominant technology for storing solar energy. They can store excess energy generated during peak sunlight hours for use during non-sunny periods. However, they face challenges related to cost, lifecycle, and environmental impact.

+ **Pumped Hydro Storage:** This method involves pumping water to a higher elevation during excess energy production and releasing it to generate electricity when needed. Although effective, it requires suitable geographical locations and significant infrastructure investment.

+ **Emerging Technologies:** Innovations such as flow batteries and solid-state batteries are being researched to provide more sustainable and efficient energy storage solutions.

High Initial Costs

The initial investment required for solar energy systems, including installation and technology development, can be prohibitive for many individuals and organizations. This financial barrier can hinder the widespread adoption of solar technologies.

Solution: Financial Incentives and Innovative Financing Models   Governments and private sectors can play a pivotal role in overcoming this barrier through:

+ **Subsidies and Tax Incentives:** Offering financial incentives such as tax credits, rebates, and grants can lower the effective cost of solar installations for consumers and businesses.

+ **Power Purchase Agreements (PPAs):** These agreements allow consumers to install solar panels with little to no upfront costs, paying for the energy produced at a predetermined rate over time.

+ **Community Solar Projects:** By pooling resources, communities can invest in larger solar installations, allowing individuals to benefit from solar energy without the burden of individual installation costs.

Grid Integration Challenges

As solar energy becomes a more significant portion of the energy mix, integrating it into existing electrical grids poses technical challenges. The grid must be able to handle the variable nature of solar energy production while maintaining stability and reliability.

Solution: Smart Grid Technologies   Investing in smart grid technologies can enhance grid management and integration. Key components include:

- **Advanced Metering Infrastructure (AMI):** Smart meters provide real-time data on energy consumption and generation, enabling better demand response and load management.

- **Distributed Energy Resources (DER) Management:**   Implementing systems that can coordinate multiple energy sources, including solar, wind, and storage, allows for more efficient energy distribution.

- **Demand Response Programs:** These programs incentivize consumers to adjust their energy usage during peak demand times, helping to balance supply and demand.

Environmental and Social Impacts

While solar energy is cleaner than fossil fuels, its production and installation can have environmental and social consequences, including land use changes, habitat disruption, and the socioeconomic effects of transitioning energy jobs.

Solution: Sustainable Practices and Community Engagement   To address these issues, stakeholders must adopt sustainable practices and engage with communities:

- **Sustainable Sourcing:**   Ensuring that materials used in solar panel production are sourced sustainably can minimize environmental impacts. This includes recycling materials and using eco-friendly manufacturing processes.

- **Community Involvement:** Engaging local communities in the planning and implementation of solar projects can help address concerns and ensure that the benefits of solar energy are equitably distributed.

+ **Job Training Programs:** As the energy landscape shifts, retraining programs for workers in fossil fuel industries can facilitate a just transition to renewable energy jobs.

Policy and Regulatory Hurdles

The regulatory landscape for renewable energy is often complex and can vary significantly between regions. Inconsistent policies can create uncertainty for investors and developers.

Solution: Comprehensive Renewable Energy Policies To foster a conducive environment for solar energy development, comprehensive policies that support renewable energy are essential:

+ **Long-term Renewable Energy Targets:** Establishing clear targets for renewable energy adoption can provide a roadmap for investment and development.

+ **Streamlined Permitting Processes:** Simplifying the regulatory process for solar installations can reduce delays and costs associated with project development.

+ **International Cooperation:** Global partnerships can facilitate knowledge sharing and technology transfer, promoting best practices in solar energy deployment.

Conclusion

Addressing the challenges of transitioning to a sustainable future powered by solar energy requires a multifaceted approach that includes technological innovation, financial strategies, policy reform, and community engagement. By implementing these solutions, society can pave the way for a cleaner, more sustainable energy landscape, ultimately fulfilling Kwame Martins's vision for a world powered by green energy.

Kwame's hope for a world powered by green energy

Kwame Martins envisions a future where green energy is not merely an alternative but the primary source of power for the entire globe. His hope is rooted in the belief that renewable energy sources, particularly solar energy, can significantly mitigate the effects of climate change, reduce reliance on fossil fuels, and create a sustainable economic framework for future generations.

The Vision of Abundant Energy

Kwame's vision is that of a world where energy is abundant, clean, and accessible to all. He often cites the equation for energy generation from solar panels, which can be expressed as:

$$E = A \cdot G \cdot \eta \tag{37}$$

where E is the energy output, A is the area of the solar panels, G is the solar irradiance (the power per unit area received from the Sun), and η is the efficiency of the solar panels.

As technology advances, Kwame believes that the efficiency η can be improved through innovative materials and designs, potentially reaching values above 30% in the near future. This would mean that solar energy can compete with and surpass traditional energy sources not only in terms of sustainability but also in cost-effectiveness.

Addressing Energy Inequity

One of Kwame's primary concerns is energy inequity. He observes that many communities, particularly in developing regions, lack reliable access to electricity. He argues that a shift to green energy can empower these communities by providing decentralized energy solutions. For instance, solar microgrids can be installed in remote areas, allowing them to harness local solar resources without the need for extensive infrastructure.

Kwame often references successful implementations of solar energy in rural Africa, where organizations like *SolarAid* have provided solar lights to households without electricity. This not only improves quality of life but also stimulates local economies by enabling small businesses to operate after dark.

The Role of Policy and Innovation

Kwame emphasizes that for his vision to materialize, strong policy frameworks must be established. He advocates for governments to implement incentives for solar energy adoption, such as tax credits and subsidies for both consumers and manufacturers. Furthermore, he believes in the importance of investing in research and development to drive innovation in renewable technologies.

For example, Kwame points to the recent advancements in perovskite solar cells, which have shown promise in achieving higher efficiencies at lower production costs. By championing such innovations, Kwame hopes to create a competitive market for renewable energy that can drive down prices and increase adoption rates.

Global Collaboration for a Sustainable Future

Kwame understands that achieving a world powered by green energy requires global collaboration. He often speaks at international conferences, advocating for a unified approach to tackling climate change. He believes that countries must work together to share technology, resources, and knowledge.

In this context, Kwame highlights the importance of initiatives like the *Paris Agreement*, which aims to unite nations in the fight against climate change. He envisions a future where countries commit to ambitious renewable energy targets, leading to a significant reduction in greenhouse gas emissions.

The Path Forward

Kwame's hope is not just a distant dream; he believes it is an achievable goal if society embraces the transition to renewable energy. He often reminds his audience that the time for change is now, and that individuals can make a difference by advocating for and adopting sustainable practices in their own lives.

In conclusion, Kwame Martins's hope for a world powered by green energy embodies a vision of sustainability, equity, and innovation. By harnessing the power of the sun, he believes humanity can create a cleaner, healthier planet for future generations. The transition to renewable energy is not merely an option; it is an imperative for survival and prosperity in the 21st century.

Conclusion

Reflecting on Kwame Martins's journey

Lessons learned and personal growth

Kwame Martins's journey through the landscape of renewable energy has been both enlightening and transformative. His experiences have imparted invaluable lessons, not only about the technical aspects of solar energy but also about the human elements that drive innovation and change.

The Power of Resilience

One of the foremost lessons Kwame learned is the importance of resilience in the face of adversity. The road to establishing Solar Solutions was fraught with challenges, including financial constraints and skepticism from established energy companies. A pivotal moment occurred during his early days when initial funding fell through, threatening the viability of his project. Instead of succumbing to despair, Kwame utilized this setback as a catalyst for innovation. He revisited his business model, sought alternative funding sources, and ultimately secured a grant from a green technology initiative. This experience taught him that failure is not the opposite of success; rather, it is a part of the journey.

Collaboration and Networking

Kwame's story underscores the significance of collaboration and building a robust support network. Early in his career, he faced the daunting task of assembling a team to bring his vision to life. He quickly realized that surrounding himself with passionate, like-minded individuals was crucial. This led him to establish connections with universities, research institutions, and industry leaders. One notable collaboration was with a local university's engineering department, where students were encouraged to contribute to the development of new solar panel designs. This partnership not only provided fresh ideas but also fostered a sense of community around the project. Kwame learned that innovation thrives in an environment of shared knowledge and collective effort.

The Importance of Education

Kwame's commitment to education has been a cornerstone of his personal growth. He often reflects on the mentors who influenced him during his formative years. Their guidance instilled in him a thirst for knowledge and a belief in the transformative power of education. This lesson manifested in his later efforts to advocate for STEM education in underserved communities. By establishing scholarships and mentorship programs, Kwame aimed to provide opportunities for young innovators who, like him, might face barriers to entry in the field of renewable energy. He believes that education is the key to unlocking potential and driving societal change.

Embracing Change and Adaptability

In the rapidly evolving field of renewable energy, Kwame learned that adaptability is essential. The technology landscape is continually shifting, with new advancements emerging at an unprecedented pace. Early in his career, he encountered a significant challenge when a competitor released a more efficient solar panel. Rather than viewing this as a setback, Kwame embraced the change, analyzing the new technology to understand its advantages. This adaptability allowed Solar Solutions to pivot its strategies and focus on developing even more innovative solutions. Kwame's experience highlights that the ability to adapt is not just a survival skill; it is a critical component of sustained success.

The Role of Advocacy

Kwame's journey also illuminated the importance of advocacy in driving systemic change. As he gained recognition in the renewable energy sector, he understood that influencing policy was crucial for the broader adoption of solar energy. He actively engaged with policymakers, sharing insights and data on the benefits of renewable energy. His advocacy efforts culminated in the successful passage of legislation that provided incentives for solar energy adoption. This experience taught him that innovation does not exist in a vacuum; it requires supportive policies and public awareness to flourish.

Personal Growth through Reflection

Finally, Kwame's journey has been marked by a commitment to self-reflection. He regularly sets aside time to evaluate his progress, reassess his goals, and identify areas for improvement. This practice has fostered a growth mindset, enabling him to view challenges as opportunities for learning. For instance, after a particularly challenging project, he conducted a thorough analysis of what went wrong and how he could improve in the future. This reflective practice has not only enhanced his leadership skills but has also inspired those around him to adopt a similar approach.

In conclusion, the lessons learned throughout Kwame Martins's journey are multifaceted and profound. Resilience, collaboration, education, adaptability, advocacy, and self-reflection have all played pivotal roles in his personal growth and the success of Solar Solutions. As he continues to innovate and inspire, these lessons serve as guiding principles for future generations of innovators in the green energy movement.

The ongoing fight for a sustainable future

The journey toward a sustainable future is not merely a personal mission for Kwame Martins; it is a collective challenge that encompasses global efforts to combat climate change, mitigate environmental degradation, and transition to renewable energy sources. The ongoing fight for sustainability is characterized by several critical dimensions, including technological innovation, policy advocacy, and grassroots mobilization.

Technological Innovation

At the heart of the transition to a sustainable future lies the need for continuous technological innovation. The development of more efficient solar panels, for instance, is essential for maximizing energy output while minimizing costs. The efficiency of solar panels can be expressed through the equation:

$$\text{Efficiency} = \frac{\text{Power Output}}{\text{Incident Solar Power}} \times 100\% \tag{38}$$

As Kwame and his team worked tirelessly to enhance the efficiency of their solar solutions, they explored novel materials such as perovskite and organic photovoltaics. These materials promise to increase efficiency rates beyond the traditional silicon-based solar cells, which typically hover around 15-20% efficiency. The potential for perovskite cells to achieve efficiencies greater than 25%

has sparked interest and investment in research, which is crucial for making solar energy a viable alternative to fossil fuels.

However, technological advancements alone are not enough. The scalability of these innovations poses a significant challenge. For instance, while a new solar technology may show promise in laboratory settings, translating that success to mass production requires addressing issues related to manufacturing processes, supply chains, and market readiness. Kwame's approach involved forming strategic partnerships with manufacturers and research institutions to ensure that innovative solutions could be scaled effectively.

Policy Advocacy

In parallel with technological advancements, advocacy for supportive policies is vital. The transition to renewable energy is heavily influenced by governmental regulations and incentives. Kwame's efforts in this arena have focused on lobbying for policies that promote solar energy adoption, such as tax credits, subsidies, and renewable energy standards.

The effectiveness of these policies can be illustrated by examining the impact of the Investment Tax Credit (ITC) in the United States, which allows homeowners and businesses to deduct a percentage of the cost of installing solar energy systems from their federal taxes. The ITC has played a pivotal role in the exponential growth of the solar industry, driving installations from a mere 1.2 gigawatts (GW) in 2008 to over 97 GW by 2020. This growth exemplifies how policy frameworks can catalyze the adoption of renewable technologies.

Grassroots Mobilization

While technological and policy advancements are crucial, the fight for sustainability also requires grassroots mobilization. Public awareness and community engagement are essential for fostering a culture of sustainability. Kwame has actively participated in educational campaigns aimed at informing the public about the benefits of solar energy, not only as a clean energy source but also as a means of economic empowerment.

Community solar projects, for example, allow individuals who may not have the means to install solar panels on their properties to benefit from solar energy. These initiatives democratize access to renewable energy and encourage community involvement in sustainability efforts. By collaborating with local organizations, Kwame has helped establish community solar farms that provide affordable energy to low-income neighborhoods, illustrating the social dimension of the sustainability movement.

Challenges Ahead

Despite the progress made, significant challenges remain in the ongoing fight for a sustainable future. The reliance on fossil fuels continues to be a major obstacle, as entrenched interests resist the transition to renewable energy. Additionally, the impacts of climate change are becoming increasingly apparent, with extreme weather events highlighting the urgency of the situation. According to the Intergovernmental Panel on Climate Change (IPCC), global greenhouse gas emissions must be halved by 2030 to limit global warming to 1.5 degrees Celsius. This goal necessitates unprecedented changes in energy production and consumption.

Moreover, the recent geopolitical tensions and economic fluctuations can disrupt supply chains for renewable technologies, hindering progress. For instance, the solar industry relies heavily on materials sourced from specific regions, and any disruption in these supply chains can lead to delays in production and increased costs.

Conclusion

The ongoing fight for a sustainable future is a multifaceted struggle that requires the collaboration of innovators, policymakers, and communities. Kwame Martins's journey exemplifies the importance of perseverance and adaptability in the face of challenges. As we strive toward a greener future, it is crucial to recognize that each step taken—whether through technological innovation, policy advocacy, or community engagement—contributes to the larger goal of a sustainable world. The path ahead may be fraught with obstacles, but the collective commitment to renewable energy and sustainability offers hope for a brighter future.

The power of perseverance and determination

In the journey of Kwame Martins, the essence of perseverance and determination stands as a beacon, illuminating the path through adversity and uncertainty. These qualities are not merely abstract ideals but are rooted in both psychological theory and practical application, serving as critical components in the pursuit of innovative solutions in the face of overwhelming challenges.

Theoretical Foundations

Psychological resilience, as defined by Masten (2001), is the capacity to recover from difficulties and adapt well to adversity. This concept is pivotal in understanding the role of perseverance in innovation. Theories of grit, popularized by psychologist Angela Duckworth, emphasize that passion and sustained persistence are crucial for achieving long-term goals. Duckworth's research indicates that grit can be a more significant predictor of success than talent or intelligence, suggesting that the relentless pursuit of a vision, despite setbacks, is fundamental to innovation.

Real-World Challenges

Kwame's journey was fraught with obstacles that tested his resolve. From financial hardships to skepticism from established energy companies, each challenge required not only technical expertise but also a steadfast commitment to his vision. For instance, during the early stages of developing Solar Solutions, Kwame faced a significant setback when a prototype failed during testing. The initial results showed an efficiency rate of only 12%, far below the industry standard of 18%. Rather than succumbing to despair, Kwame utilized this failure as a learning opportunity, conducting a thorough analysis of the materials and design flaws.

$$\text{Efficiency}_{new} = \frac{\text{Power Output}_{new}}{\text{Solar Input}} \times 100 \qquad (39)$$

This equation became a mantra for his team, emphasizing the importance of iterative testing and improvement. The determination to enhance the efficiency of the solar panels led to innovative breakthroughs in material science, ultimately achieving an efficiency rate of 22% within two years.

Examples of Perseverance

Kwame's story is replete with instances of perseverance. One notable example occurred when he sought funding from venture capitalists who were initially uninterested in renewable energy projects. After multiple rejections, he organized a grassroots campaign to raise awareness about the benefits of solar energy. By leveraging social media platforms, he was able to gather a following that demonstrated public interest and support for his vision. This not only attracted the attention of potential investors but also illustrated the power of community engagement in driving change.

The Impact of Determination

Kwame's determination also extended to advocating for policy changes that would benefit the renewable energy sector. He faced numerous legislative hurdles, often encountering opposition from powerful fossil fuel interests. However, his unwavering commitment to education and advocacy led to the successful lobbying of a bill that provided tax incentives for solar energy installations. This legislative win not only benefited his company but also set a precedent that encouraged other innovators in the field.

Lessons Learned

The journey of Kwame Martins exemplifies the profound impact of perseverance and determination in the realm of innovation. The lessons learned from his experiences resonate with the broader narrative of the renewable energy movement. As highlighted by Dweck's (2006) concept of a growth mindset, the belief that abilities can be developed through dedication and hard work is crucial for overcoming obstacles. Kwame's ability to maintain focus on his long-term goals, despite immediate challenges, serves as a powerful reminder that resilience is a key driver of success.

In conclusion, the power of perseverance and determination is not just a personal attribute but a collective force that propels innovators like Kwame Martins toward transformative solutions. It is through the lens of these qualities that we can appreciate the ongoing fight for a sustainable future, recognizing that every setback is a setup for a comeback. The journey toward clean energy is paved with challenges, but it is the determination to persist that will ultimately lead to a brighter, greener world.

Acknowledgments

Thanking those who supported Kwame Martins along the way

Mentors, advisors, and colleagues

The journey of Kwame Martins would not have been possible without the invaluable contributions of mentors, advisors, and colleagues who played pivotal roles in his development as a green energy pioneer. Their guidance, support, and expertise helped shape his vision for Solar Solutions and enabled him to navigate the complex landscape of renewable energy.

The Role of Mentorship

Mentorship is a critical component of personal and professional growth, particularly in fields that require specialized knowledge and innovative thinking. According to Kram (1985), mentorship can be defined as a relationship in which a more experienced individual provides guidance, support, and advice to a less experienced individual. This relationship is characterized by mutual respect and a commitment to the mentee's development. In Kwame's case, he was fortunate to have several mentors who recognized his potential and offered their insights into the renewable energy sector.

One of Kwame's most significant mentors was Dr. Angela Reyes, a leading researcher in solar technology. Dr. Reyes introduced Kwame to advanced concepts in photovoltaic systems and encouraged him to pursue research opportunities during his undergraduate studies. Her emphasis on the importance of empirical data and rigorous testing laid the foundation for Kwame's approach to developing solar panels. For instance, she often quoted the maxim:

$$E = mc^2 \tag{40}$$

This equation, while primarily associated with physics, became a metaphor for Kwame. It represented the energy (E) that could be derived from mass (m) through innovative processes (c) in renewable energy technology. Dr. Reyes instilled in Kwame the belief that with the right approach, solar energy could be harnessed effectively to meet global demands.

Advisors in the Business Realm

In addition to academic mentorship, Kwame sought guidance from advisors in the business realm. One such advisor was Mr. Samuel Greene, a seasoned entrepreneur with extensive experience in the energy sector. Mr. Greene provided Kwame with insights into the challenges of securing funding and navigating the competitive landscape of renewable energy startups. He emphasized the importance of developing a solid business plan, which would include market analysis, financial projections, and a clear value proposition.

To illustrate the significance of a well-structured business model, Mr. Greene introduced Kwame to the Business Model Canvas, a strategic management tool that allows entrepreneurs to visualize their business model on a single page. This tool helped Kwame articulate his vision for Solar Solutions and identify key partners, activities, and resources necessary for success.

Collaborative Efforts with Colleagues

Kwame's journey was also marked by the collaborative efforts of his colleagues, who shared his passion for renewable energy. The formation of a diverse team was crucial in fostering innovation and creativity. Each team member brought unique skills and perspectives, enabling Solar Solutions to tackle complex problems more effectively.

For example, Dr. Lisa Chen, a materials scientist, played a vital role in the research and development of new solar panel materials. Her expertise in nanotechnology led to significant breakthroughs in the efficiency and durability of solar cells. Under her guidance, the team was able to develop a prototype that increased the efficiency of solar panels by 30%, a remarkable achievement that garnered attention from industry leaders.

Moreover, Kwame's collaboration with engineers, marketing specialists, and environmental scientists fostered a holistic approach to problem-solving. This interdisciplinary teamwork exemplified the concept of collective intelligence, where the combined knowledge and skills of a group exceed the capabilities of individual members. As stated by Surowiecki (2004), "The wisdom of crowds" can lead to innovative solutions that might not be achievable through isolated efforts.

The Impact of Support Networks

The support networks that Kwame cultivated throughout his career were instrumental in overcoming obstacles. These networks included professional organizations, academic institutions, and community groups dedicated to promoting renewable energy. For instance, Kwame joined the Solar Energy Society, where he connected with other professionals in the field, attended conferences, and exchanged ideas on best practices in solar technology.

Networking also played a crucial role in securing funding for Solar Solutions. Through connections made at industry events, Kwame was able to pitch his vision to potential investors, ultimately leading to the initial funding necessary to launch his startup. This experience underscores the importance of building relationships within one's industry, as highlighted by Granovetter (1973) in his theory of weak ties, which suggests that connections outside of one's immediate social circle can provide access to valuable resources and opportunities.

Conclusion

In conclusion, the contributions of mentors, advisors, and colleagues were fundamental to Kwame Martins's success as a green energy pioneer. Their guidance, expertise, and support not only shaped his technical knowledge but also instilled the confidence and resilience necessary to navigate the challenges of the renewable energy sector. As Kwame reflects on his journey, he recognizes that the collaborative spirit and shared vision of those around him were crucial in transforming his dream of a sustainable future into a reality. The lessons learned from these relationships continue to inspire him as he advocates for clean energy solutions and empowers the next generation of innovators.

Family and friends

Kwame Martins's journey to becoming a green energy pioneer was not solely a product of his own ambition and intellect; it was also significantly shaped by the unwavering support of his family and friends. In this section, we will explore how these relationships provided him with the emotional and practical backing necessary to navigate the challenges of his career and how they contributed to his overall success.

The Role of Family

Kwame's family played a pivotal role in his early life, instilling in him the values of hard work, resilience, and the importance of education. His parents, immigrants who faced their own struggles, emphasized the necessity of academic achievement as a pathway to a better life. This foundational belief not only motivated Kwame to excel in school but also nurtured his passion for science and technology.

For instance, Kwame's mother often recounted stories of their homeland, where access to electricity was a luxury rather than a standard. This narrative ignited a fire in Kwame to pursue solutions that could bring energy to underserved communities. The emotional weight of his family's experiences with energy scarcity became a driving force behind his commitment to renewable energy.

Furthermore, Kwame's siblings were instrumental in providing a supportive environment. They celebrated his academic achievements and provided encouragement during times of doubt. This familial support network was crucial when Kwame faced setbacks, such as failed prototypes or funding rejections. The encouragement from his family helped him maintain his focus and determination, reminding him of the larger mission at hand.

Friendship and Collaboration

In addition to family, Kwame's friendships also played a significant role in his journey. Many of his closest friends shared similar aspirations and values, creating a community of like-minded individuals committed to innovation and sustainability. This network not only provided emotional support but also facilitated collaboration on projects and ideas.

One notable example is his friendship with fellow engineering student, Maya Chen, who shared Kwame's passion for renewable energy. Together, they worked on various projects during their college years, including a solar-powered water heater that won a university innovation award. Their partnership exemplified how collaboration can lead to breakthroughs that might not be possible in isolation.

Moreover, Kwame's friends often acted as a sounding board for his ideas. They provided constructive criticism and alternative perspectives that helped him refine his vision for Solar Solutions. This collaborative spirit extended beyond his immediate circle, as Kwame actively sought out relationships with other innovators in the renewable energy space. These connections led to partnerships that were instrumental in the growth of his company.

Emotional Resilience

The emotional support Kwame received from his family and friends was crucial in building his resilience. The journey of an entrepreneur, particularly in the renewable energy sector, is fraught with challenges, including skepticism from traditional energy companies and regulatory hurdles. During moments of doubt, such as when his initial funding application was rejected, Kwame turned to his family and friends for encouragement.

For example, after a particularly difficult week, Kwame's best friend organized a small gathering to lift his spirits. This act of kindness reminded Kwame that he was not alone in his struggles and that he had a support system ready to rally behind him. Such moments of solidarity reinforced his resolve to continue pursuing his goals, even when the path was not clear.

Legacy of Support

Kwame's success is a testament to the power of community and the importance of nurturing relationships. As he reflects on his journey, he acknowledges that the support from his family and friends was not just a backdrop to his achievements; it was an integral part of his story. Their belief in his vision and their willingness to stand by him during challenging times were vital to his development as a leader in the green energy movement.

In conclusion, the contributions of family and friends to Kwame Martins's journey cannot be overstated. Their support provided the emotional and practical foundation necessary for him to pursue his dreams. As Kwame continues to innovate and inspire others in the renewable energy sector, he carries with him the lessons learned from those who believed in him from the very beginning. Their influence will undoubtedly shape his legacy as a pioneer in green energy.

The readers and supporters of his work

Kwame Martins's journey in the realm of green energy has been significantly shaped by the unwavering support of readers and advocates who resonate with his vision for a sustainable future. These individuals, ranging from eco-conscious consumers to budding scientists and activists, have played a crucial role in amplifying his message and fostering a community dedicated to the advancement of renewable energy solutions.

The Role of Readers

Readers are not merely passive consumers of Kwame's work; they are active participants in the dialogue surrounding renewable energy. Their engagement with his writings—whether through books, articles, or social media posts—creates a ripple effect, encouraging others to consider the implications of energy consumption and the potential of solar solutions. This engagement can be understood through the lens of the *Diffusion of Innovations* theory, which posits that new ideas and technologies spread through specific channels over time, influenced by the characteristics of the adopters.

The adoption curve can be represented mathematically as:

$$P(t) = \frac{P_{max}}{1 + e^{-k(t-t_0)}} \tag{41}$$

where $P(t)$ is the number of adopters at time t, P_{max} is the maximum potential adopters, k is the rate of adoption, and t_0 is the inflection point of the curve. Kwame's readers often find themselves in the early adopter category, eager to embrace innovative solutions that promise environmental benefits.

Community Building

Supporters of Kwame's work extend beyond mere readership; they form a community that actively engages in discussions, workshops, and initiatives that promote solar energy. This community is characterized by a shared vision of a sustainable future, where renewable energy is accessible and affordable for all. The power of community is evident in grassroots movements that have emerged in response to Kwame's advocacy.

For instance, local organizations have started initiatives to educate communities about the benefits of solar energy, often using Kwame's work as a foundational resource. These initiatives can be quantified by measuring participation rates and the subsequent increase in solar panel installations within those communities.

The Importance of Feedback

The relationship between Kwame and his supporters is reciprocal; while Kwame provides knowledge and inspiration, the feedback from his readers helps refine his ideas and strategies. This feedback loop is essential for continuous improvement and innovation in the field of renewable energy. It can be illustrated through the *Feedback Loop Theory*, which emphasizes the importance of input and output in any system.

$$F = I - O \tag{42}$$

where F is the feedback, I is the input (ideas and support from readers), and O is the output (the initiatives and innovations produced). A positive feedback loop results in enhanced motivation for both Kwame and his supporters, driving further advancements in solar technology.

Examples of Impact

The impact of Kwame's supporters is evident in various projects that have emerged as a direct result of his influence. For instance, a community-driven solar initiative in a rural area led to the installation of solar panels on local schools, significantly reducing energy costs and providing educational opportunities related to renewable energy. This project serves as a case study in the potential for community engagement to drive change, demonstrating the tangible benefits of Kwame's work and the commitment of his supporters.

Conclusion

In conclusion, the readers and supporters of Kwame Martins's work are integral to the advancement of green energy solutions. Their engagement, feedback, and community-building efforts not only amplify his message but also contribute to a broader movement towards sustainability. As Kwame continues to innovate and inspire, the collective efforts of his supporters will undoubtedly play a pivotal role in shaping the future of renewable energy.

Appendix

Glossary of terms

Definitions of key terms related to renewable energy

In this section, we will define key terms that are fundamental to understanding the field of renewable energy. Each term will be explained with relevant theories, problems, and examples to provide a comprehensive overview.

Renewable Energy

Renewable energy refers to energy that is generated from natural processes that are continuously replenished. This includes sources such as solar, wind, hydroelectric, geothermal, and biomass energy. Unlike fossil fuels, which are finite and contribute to environmental degradation, renewable energy sources have a lower environmental impact and can contribute to sustainable development.

Solar Energy

Solar energy is the energy harnessed from the sun's radiation. It can be converted into thermal or electrical energy using various technologies. The most common methods include photovoltaic (PV) systems and solar thermal systems.

$$E = A \cdot G \cdot \eta \tag{43}$$

Where:

- E = energy produced (kWh)

- A = area of the solar panel (m²)

- G = solar irradiance (kW/m²)

+ η = efficiency of the solar panel (as a decimal)

Photovoltaic (PV) Cells

Photovoltaic cells are devices that convert sunlight directly into electricity through the photovoltaic effect. When light photons strike the surface of the PV cell, they excite electrons, creating an electric current.

Wind Energy

Wind energy is generated by harnessing the kinetic energy of moving air. Wind turbines convert this kinetic energy into mechanical power, which can then be converted into electricity. The power generated by a wind turbine can be expressed as:

$$P = \frac{1}{2} \cdot \rho \cdot A \cdot v^3 \tag{44}$$

Where:

+ P = power (W)

+ ρ = air density (kg/m³)

+ A = swept area of the turbine blades (m²)

+ v = wind speed (m/s)

Hydroelectric Power

Hydroelectric power is generated by the movement of water, typically through dams on rivers. The potential energy of stored water is converted into kinetic energy, which turns turbines to generate electricity.

The power output from a hydroelectric plant can be calculated using:

$$P = \eta \cdot \rho \cdot g \cdot h \cdot Q \tag{45}$$

Where:

+ P = power (W)

+ η = efficiency of the turbine (as a decimal)

+ ρ = density of water (kg/m³)

+ g = acceleration due to gravity (9.81 m/s²)

+ h = height of the water fall (m)

+ Q = flow rate of water (m³/s)

Geothermal Energy

Geothermal energy is derived from the heat stored beneath the Earth's surface. This energy can be harnessed for direct heating or to generate electricity. Geothermal power plants typically use steam from heated water reservoirs to turn turbines.

Biomass Energy

Biomass energy is produced from organic materials, such as plant and animal waste. It can be converted into biofuels or used directly for heating. Biomass is considered renewable because it can be replenished through sustainable practices.

Energy Efficiency

Energy efficiency refers to using less energy to perform the same task or produce the same outcome. Improving energy efficiency can reduce energy consumption and lower greenhouse gas emissions. Common examples include LED lighting, energy-efficient appliances, and improved insulation in buildings.

Carbon Footprint

A carbon footprint is the total amount of greenhouse gases (GHGs) emitted directly or indirectly by an individual, organization, event, or product, usually expressed in equivalent tons of carbon dioxide (CO_2). Reducing one's carbon footprint is essential for mitigating climate change.

Net Metering

Net metering is a billing arrangement that allows solar energy system owners to receive credit for the electricity they generate and feed back into the grid. This system encourages the adoption of renewable energy by making it more economically viable for homeowners and businesses.

Sustainability

Sustainability refers to the ability to meet present needs without compromising the ability of future generations to meet their own needs. In the context of energy, sustainability involves transitioning to renewable energy sources and promoting energy efficiency to minimize environmental impact.

Energy Transition

Energy transition is the process of shifting from fossil fuel-based energy systems to renewable energy systems. This transition is driven by the need to reduce greenhouse gas emissions and combat climate change while ensuring energy security and access for all.

Smart Grid

A smart grid is an electricity supply network that uses digital communication technology to detect and react to local changes in usage. It allows for better integration of renewable energy sources, improves reliability, and enhances energy efficiency.

Energy Storage

Energy storage refers to technologies that capture and store energy for use at a later time. This is crucial for renewable energy sources like solar and wind, which are intermittent by nature. Common energy storage technologies include batteries, pumped hydro storage, and thermal storage.

Distributed Energy Resources (DER)

Distributed Energy Resources are small-scale units of local generation connected to the grid at the distribution level. Examples include rooftop solar panels, small wind turbines, and energy storage systems. DERs enhance grid resilience and promote energy independence.

Life Cycle Assessment (LCA)

Life Cycle Assessment is a method for assessing the environmental impacts associated with all stages of a product's life, from raw material extraction through production, use, and disposal. LCA is crucial for understanding the overall sustainability of renewable energy technologies.

Decarbonization

Decarbonization refers to the process of reducing carbon dioxide emissions associated with energy production and consumption. This involves transitioning to renewable energy sources, improving energy efficiency, and implementing carbon capture and storage technologies.

Feed-in Tariff (FiT)

A Feed-in Tariff is a policy mechanism designed to encourage the adoption of renewable energy by guaranteeing fixed payments to energy producers for the electricity they generate and feed into the grid. This provides a stable income for renewable energy projects and promotes investment.

Greenhouse Gas (GHG) Emissions

Greenhouse gases are gases that trap heat in the atmosphere, contributing to the greenhouse effect and climate change. Major GHGs include carbon dioxide (CO_2), methane (CH_4), and nitrous oxide (N_2O). Reducing GHG emissions is a key goal of renewable energy initiatives.

Energy Independence

Energy independence refers to the ability of a country or region to meet its energy needs without relying on external sources. Achieving energy independence often involves increasing the use of domestic renewable energy resources and reducing dependence on fossil fuels.

Carbon Neutrality

Carbon neutrality is the state of having a net-zero carbon footprint, achieved by balancing emitted carbon with an equivalent amount of carbon removal or offsets. Many organizations and countries are setting targets for carbon neutrality as part of their climate action plans.

Through these definitions, we can better understand the critical concepts that underpin the renewable energy sector and the importance of transitioning to sustainable energy solutions. By familiarizing ourselves with these terms, we equip ourselves with the knowledge necessary to engage in discussions about renewable energy and its role in addressing the world's energy crisis.

Organizations and initiatives supporting clean energy

The transition to clean energy is not solely the responsibility of individual innovators like Kwame Martins; it is a collective effort supported by numerous organizations and initiatives worldwide. These entities play a crucial role in promoting, developing, and implementing renewable energy technologies, advocating for policy changes, and educating the public about sustainable practices. Below are some of the key organizations and initiatives that are at the forefront of the clean energy movement.

International Renewable Energy Agency (IRENA)

IRENA is an intergovernmental organization that supports countries in their transition to sustainable energy. Established in 2009, its mission is to promote the widespread adoption and sustainable use of renewable energy. IRENA provides a platform for collaboration, knowledge sharing, and capacity building among its member states.

Key Contributions:

+ *Data and Analysis:* IRENA publishes comprehensive reports and data sets that analyze the current state of renewable energy technologies, their economic viability, and their potential impact on global energy markets.

+ *Policy Advocacy:* The agency works with governments to develop policies that facilitate the integration of renewable energy into national energy systems.

+ *Capacity Building:* IRENA provides training and resources to help countries develop their renewable energy capabilities.

World Resources Institute (WRI)

The WRI is a global research organization that focuses on sustainable development and environmental issues. It conducts research, develops policy recommendations, and engages with businesses and governments to promote sustainable practices.

Key Contributions:

+ *Research and Insights:* WRI conducts in-depth research on the impact of energy systems on the environment, including studies on greenhouse gas emissions and the potential of renewable energy sources.

+ *Initiatives:* The organization leads initiatives such as the Global Forest Watch and the Aqueduct Water Risk Atlas, which incorporate renewable energy considerations into broader environmental assessments.

+ *Engagement with Corporations:* WRI collaborates with companies to help them transition to renewable energy, providing tools and frameworks for corporate sustainability.

The Solar Foundation

The Solar Foundation is a nonprofit organization dedicated to advancing solar energy through education, research, and advocacy. It aims to increase the adoption of solar technologies and enhance the solar workforce.

Key Contributions:

+ *National Solar Jobs Census:* The Solar Foundation conducts an annual census that tracks the growth of solar jobs in the United States, providing valuable data for policymakers and industry stakeholders.

+ *Education and Training:* The organization offers training programs and resources to help individuals gain the skills necessary for careers in the solar industry.

+ *Advocacy:* The Solar Foundation advocates for policies that support solar energy development, including tax incentives and renewable energy standards.

Clean Energy States Alliance (CESA)

CESA is a coalition of public agencies and organizations that work together to promote clean energy technologies. The alliance focuses on state-level initiatives and policies that encourage the adoption of renewable energy.

Key Contributions:

+ *Collaboration and Networking:* CESA facilitates collaboration among states to share best practices and innovative solutions for clean energy deployment.

+ *Policy Development:* The organization assists states in developing and implementing clean energy policies and programs, including renewable portfolio standards and energy efficiency initiatives.

+ *Research and Reports:* CESA produces reports that analyze state-level clean energy programs and their effectiveness in achieving renewable energy goals.

Green Climate Fund (GCF)

The GCF is a global fund established to support the efforts of developing countries to respond to climate change. It aims to promote low-emission and climate-resilient development pathways.

Key Contributions:

+ *Funding Projects:* The GCF provides financial assistance for projects that promote renewable energy, energy efficiency, and sustainable development in developing countries.

+ *Capacity Building:* The fund supports capacity-building initiatives to help countries develop their renewable energy sectors and improve their resilience to climate impacts.

+ *Partnerships:* GCF collaborates with various stakeholders, including governments, private sector actors, and civil society organizations, to enhance the effectiveness of climate finance.

Local Initiatives

In addition to global and national organizations, numerous local initiatives are essential to promoting clean energy at the community level. These initiatives often focus on specific projects, such as community solar programs, energy efficiency upgrades, and local advocacy efforts.

Examples:

+ *Community Solar Projects:* These projects allow multiple community members to invest in and benefit from a shared solar installation, making solar energy more accessible to those who cannot install panels on their properties.

+ *Local Nonprofits:* Many local nonprofits focus on renewable energy education, helping residents understand the benefits of clean energy and how to implement it in their homes and businesses.

+ *Municipal Programs:* Cities and towns are increasingly adopting renewable energy goals, creating programs to support energy efficiency, solar installations, and electric vehicle adoption within their communities.

Conclusion

Organizations and initiatives supporting clean energy are vital to the global transition towards a sustainable future. Their collective efforts in research, advocacy, education, and funding help overcome the barriers to renewable energy adoption. By collaborating with innovators like Kwame Martins, these organizations can amplify their impact and drive meaningful change in the energy landscape. The challenges of climate change and energy security require a concerted effort from all sectors of society, and these organizations are leading the charge toward a cleaner, more sustainable world.

Author's note

Reflecting on the writing process and inspiration behind the book

Writing "Green Energy Pioneer: Kwame Martins's Solar Solutions" has been an enlightening journey, one that has deepened my understanding of renewable energy and the innovative minds that drive progress in this field. The inspiration for this book stemmed from a desire to highlight the stories of individuals who are not just dreaming of a sustainable future but actively working to create it. Kwame Martins is a fictional character, yet his journey embodies the real struggles and triumphs faced by countless innovators in the green energy sector.

The writing process began with extensive research into the current state of renewable energy technologies, particularly solar energy. I immersed myself in literature, scientific journals, and case studies, seeking to understand the challenges and breakthroughs that define this industry. This foundational knowledge was crucial, as it allowed me to create a narrative that is both compelling and informative. I aimed to balance technical accuracy with accessibility, ensuring that readers from diverse backgrounds could appreciate the significance of Kwame's work.

One of the key theories that guided my writing was the concept of the "innovation cycle." This theory posits that innovation is not a linear process but rather a cyclical one, characterized by phases of inspiration, experimentation, failure, and eventual success. As I chronicled Kwame's journey, I aimed to illustrate this cycle, emphasizing that setbacks are not merely obstacles but essential components of the innovation process. For example, in Chapter Two, I detailed the initial skepticism Kwame faced from traditional energy companies. This resistance, rather than deterring him, fueled his determination to prove the viability of solar energy solutions.

Another significant aspect of the writing process was the integration of real-world examples of solar energy pioneers. I drew inspiration from figures such as Elon Musk, whose work with solar technologies and electric vehicles has reshaped public perceptions of renewable energy. By weaving these real stories into Kwame's narrative, I aimed to create a sense of authenticity while also inspiring readers to believe in the potential for change.

Throughout the writing process, I encountered several challenges, particularly in how to effectively communicate complex scientific concepts. To address this, I employed various strategies, such as using analogies and visual aids. For instance, when discussing the efficiency of solar panels, I compared it to the way a sponge absorbs water, making the concept more relatable. Additionally, I included equations, such as the efficiency formula:

$$\text{Efficiency}(\eta) = \frac{\text{Output Power}}{\text{Input Power}} \times 100\%$$

This equation not only provided a quantitative measure of solar panel performance but also reinforced the importance of scientific rigor in the narrative.

Moreover, I was mindful of the broader implications of Kwame's story. The transition to renewable energy is not just a technological challenge; it is also a social and political one. In Chapter Four, I explored the role of advocacy in influencing policy and public opinion, highlighting how Kwame's efforts to lobby for renewable energy legislation were essential in overcoming systemic barriers. This aspect of the narrative serves as a reminder that innovation is often intertwined with activism, and that the fight for a sustainable future requires not only technical solutions but also societal change.

As I reflect on the writing process, I am struck by the transformative power of storytelling. By crafting Kwame's biography, I sought to inspire readers to envision themselves as agents of change. I hope that his journey resonates with those who feel passionate about environmental issues, encouraging them to pursue their own paths in the green energy movement.

In conclusion, the writing of "Green Energy Pioneer: Kwame Martins's Solar Solutions" has been a deeply rewarding experience, one that has reinforced my belief in the power of innovation and perseverance. Through Kwame's story, I aspire to illuminate the challenges and triumphs of those who dare to dream of a sustainable future, ultimately inspiring a new generation of innovators to take up the mantle of change.

Index